Detroit Monographs in Musicology/Studies in Music, No. 48

Editor
Susan Parisi
University of Illinois

Further Revelations of an Opera Manager in 19th Century America

The Third Book of Memoirs
by Max Maretzek

Edited and Annotated
by Ruth Henderson

Harmonie Park Press
Sterling Heights, Michigan 2006

Cover:

TEATRO TACÓN, Havana, interior, wood engraving,
from Samuel Hazard, *Cuba with Pen and Pencil*
(Hartford: Hartford Pub. Co., 1871), facing p. 186.
This figure also appears on page 40 of this book.

Courtesy of the General Research Division, New York Public Library
and the Astor, Lenox, and Tilden Foundations

Printed and bound in the United States of America
Published by
Harmonie Park Press
Liberty Professional Center
35675 Mound Road
Sterling Heights, Michigan 48310-4727

Publications Director, Elaine Gorzelski
Editor, Susan Parisi
Cover design, Mitchell Groters
Book design and Typographer, Colleen McRorie

Library of Congress Cataloging-in-Publication Data

Maretzek, Max, 1821-1897.
　　Further revelations of an opera manager in 19th century America : the third book of
　　memoirs / by Max Maretzek ; edited and annotated by Ruth Henderson.
　　　　p. cm — (Detroit monographs in musicology/Studies in music ; no. 48)
　　Includes bibliographical references (p.) and index.
　　ISBN 0-89990-135-2
　　1. Maretzek, Max, 1821-1897. 2. Opera producers and directors—United
States—Biography. 3. Opera companies—United States—History—19th century. I.
Henderson, Ruth, 1943- II. Title. III. Series.

ML429.M32A3 2006
792.5'023092—dc22
[B]

2006043542

CONTENTS

ILLUSTRATIONS

Figures

PREFACE

Max Maretzek's two spirited books of published memoirs offer an invaluable window on the emerging profession of opera management in New York during the third quarter of the nineteenth century. The first, *Crotchets and Quavers*, published in 1855, was reissued by Da Capo in 1966 and again in 1968 by Dover, together with the second book, *Sharps and Flats*, originally published in 1890, and accompanied by an extensive introduction by Charles Haywood.

This volume presents yet a third (incomplete) book by Maretzek which surfaced in 1981 and is published here for the first time.[1] It encompasses primarily the years from 1862 to 1867 and focuses on the activities of Maretzek and his various companies in their home city, New York. Spelling and punctuation have been corrected and headings, including the title, "Further Revelations" added, but the third book is otherwise reproduced as Maretzek wrote it. Summaries of the first two books precede it. Material from contemporary sources that corroborates and embellishes the original, particularly reviews from major New York newspapers and *Dwight's Journal of Music*, has been added (together with dates, infrequent in all three books), to supplement Maretzek's account. I am indebted to Vera Brodsky Lawrence's *Strong on Music* (which extends through 1862), as well as to William Templeton Strong himself, whose remarkable diary provides the framework for her study. Considering Maretzek's pivotal role in the establishment of Italian opera in New York, it is curious that no book-length biography of him has yet appeared. I hope that the present study will help to fill this gap.

I am indebted to George Del Grosso, the owner of the Maretzek manuscript and of other Maretzek archival materials, for allowing me access to his collection. He graciously welcomed me from the day in the fall of 1998 when I appeared

---

[1] Henry C. Lahee alludes to this third volume in his *Grand Opera in America* (Freeport, NY: Books for Libraries, 1971), 90.

unannounced at his door through several return visits. These materials would not have survived had he and his family not chosen to preserve and care for them. I am also grateful to Mrs. Carol Kennedy, Maretzek's great grand-daughter, for her interest in this volume and for sharing early family memories with me.

Several colleagues at The City College of New York made particular contributions to the project that I wish here to mention. To John Graziano of the Music Department, I express my heartfelt thanks for his encouragement and guidance, as well as for the innumerable suggestions and advice he gave me on countless matters. I warmly thank my colleagues in the City College Library, particularly Pamela Gillespie, Robert Laurich, Sara J. Lyon, Richard Uttich, Sydney Van Nort, and the staff of the Interlibrary Loan Division, for their assistance. A fellowship leave and a professional reassignment leave from the College Library greatly facilitated my work on this book. I also gratefully acknowledge the contributions of my friend, the late Paul David Pearson of the School of Architecture, who shared my fascination with New York's past.

The treasures of The New York Public Library were an invaluable resource. I thank the librarians of the Music Division, particularly Susan T. Sommer and Fran Barulich, as well as the personnel in the Humanities and Social Sciences Library, including General Research, Rare Books, Maps, the Dorot Jewish Division, Microforms Reading Room, and the St. George (Staten Island) Branch Library. I also wish to express my appreciation to the following librarians and archivists for their assistance: Barbara Haws, New York Philharmonic Archives; Barbara File, Metropolitan Museum of Art Library, who put me in touch with Carol Kennedy, whom I had despaired of ever locating after she married in 1948 (changing her surname from Maretzek) and moved to the West Coast; Carlotta DeFillo, Staten Island Historical Society Library, where I encountered an article in the *Staten Island Advance* describing Maretzek's manuscript for his third book of memoirs; the reference librarians at The New York Historical Society Library and Kristine Paulus of the Department of Prints; the personnel at the Columbia University Libraries, particularly Elizabeth Davis, Music Librarian; Tara Craig of the Rare Book and Manuscript Library; and the staff of the Microforms Reading Room.

I would also like to record my debt to Allen Lott, for his assistance with elusive illustrations at the Bibliothèque Nationale, Paris; Dena Epstein, whose comment in a review of a volume of Vera Brodsky Lawrence's *Strong on Music* piqued my curiosity about impresarios in nineteenth-century New York; and to Lawrence Lerner and Mimi Daitz. Finally, I would like to thank the late J. Bunker Clark and Susan Parisi, series editors; Colleen McRorie, typographer; and Elaine Gorzelski, publications director, of Harmonie Park Press, for guiding this book through production.

RUTH HENDERSON

New York City
Spring 2005

ABBREVIATIONS

C&Q   *Crotchets and Quavers, or Revelations of an Opera Manager in America by Max Maretzek* (New York, 1855). Dover Reprint Edition (under alternate title, *Revelations of an Opera Manager in 19th-Century America*, with a new introduction by Charles Haywood), New York, 1968.

S&F   *Sharps and Flats* (New York, 1980). Dover Edition (with *Crotchets and Quavers*, under alternate title as noted above), New York, 1968.

Further Revelations of an Opera Manager in 19th Century America

The Third Book of Memoirs
by Max Maretzek

INTRODUCTION

In the summer of 1948, a painting contractor clearing out the attic of the ninety-eight-year-old widow of a Staten Island grocer came across several cartons of memorabilia. The boxes of old newspaper clippings, letters, and writings piqued his interest, and he put them aside for safe-keeping in his basement, where they remained until his death nearly twenty-seven years later. The widow was Marie A. Wilbur, eldest daughter of Max Maretzek (maRETzek),[1] opera impresario, conductor, and composer active in New York during the third quarter of the nineteenth century.

Max Maretzek played a prominent role in the establishment of Italian opera in the United States. His two books of memoirs, *Crotchets and Quavers*, published in 1855 (the Anglicized terms for quarter and eighth notes), and *Sharps and Flats*, published in 1890, afford a lively glimpse into the sometimes-cutthroat world of opera management during this era.[2] Among the papers in the painting contractor's basement was an eighty-six-page handwritten manuscript on lined, 8 x 12 ½ inch paper for a third book of memoirs, still incomplete at Maretzek's death in 1897. It first came to the attention of scholars in 1981, when the painter's son, who inherited the memorabilia, had it authenticated and appraised for

---

[1] This is the pronunciation given by Maretzek's great granddaughter, Carol H. Kennedy (née Maretzek). In Czech, however, the accent would have fallen on the first syllable, and the last syllable would have been pronounced "check" (original spelling: Mareczek); see "A Note on Czech Pronunciation" in Derek Sayer, *The Coasts of Bohemia: A Czech History* (Princeton: Princeton University Press, 1998). A comment from a review suggests that Maretzek may have followed this pronunciation more closely: an audience, demanding his appearance, chanted "Maretzek! Check! Retchek! Maxmerechek!" Max Maretzek, *Sharps and Flats* (New York: Dover, 1968), 24.

[2] Max Maretzek, *Crotchets and Quavers or Revelations of an Opera Manager in America* (New York: French, 1855; reprint Da Capo, 1966); reprint New York: Dover, 1968, together with Maretzek's second book, *Sharps and Flats* (New York: American Publishing Company, 1890), under the alternate title, *Revelations of an Opera Manager in 19th-Century America*, and with an introduction by Charles Haywood.

possible sale. It then lay undisturbed in his attic for another twenty-five years until its publication here for the first time. That it survived at all and in such excellent condition, is thanks to the care of the Staten Island painter and his family who recognized in it something of value and chose to preserve it.[3]

Max Maretzek (fig. 1), born Maximilian Mareczek on 28 June 1821, in Brünn (now Brno), Moravia, then a province of the Austrian Empire and now in the Czech Republic, studied piano as a boy, but, following his parents' wishes, pursued a course of study first in medicine, and then law at the University of Vienna. Finding neither field appealing as a career, however, he returned to music, with the encouragement of another Moravian who had originally aspired to a career in medicine: music historian, pianist, and composer Joseph Fischhof (to whom Maretzek's fourth letter in *Crotchets and Quavers* is addressed). Fischhof also preceded Maretzek in composition studies under composer and conductor Ignaz Xaver Ritter von Seyfried, who had studied piano with Mozart.[4] Maretzek oversaw the production and conducted the premiere of his own first mature opera, *Hamlet*, in Brno on 5 November 1840, and subsequently held conducting posts in Bratislava, Slovakia; Zagreb, Croatia; Bamberg and Nuremberg, Germany; and Nancy, France. He continued to compose and conduct in Paris, where he relocated in 1842.[5] He was made choral director and assistant director at Her Majesty's Theatre in Covent Garden, London, in 1844 and chorus master at Drury Lane in 1847. He addressed his first letter in *Crotchets and Quavers* to Hector Berlioz, who was conductor at Drury Lane during Maretzek's tenure there. The two roomed together, and Maretzek later described him as moody, gloomy, and lovesick, as well as "one of the most lovable fellows" he ever met. Louis Jullien's ambitious plan for presenting opera in English at Drury Lane collapsed after a few months, and Maretzek was compelled to seek his living from freelance work.[6]

---

[3] The discovery was made by Julius Del Grosso; see Douglas Patrick, "Stapleton Man Hits High C with Historic Find," *Staten Island Advance*, 13 December 1981, pp. A1, A4.

[4] Maretzek had begged Fischhof to intervene with his parents and credits Fischhof with gaining their acquiescence to his pursuit of a career in music: *Crotchets and Quavers* [hereafter, *C&Q*], 139, 146.

[5] Before moving to Paris, Maretzek had composed a second opera, *Die Nibelungen*, a grand romantic opera in five acts that was never produced in its entirety. In Paris, he began writing polkas, waltzes, songs, and ballet music. After moving to London he published about thirty waltzes, quadrilles, and songs, wrote three ballets, produced at Her Majesty's Theatre, and a third opera, *Riccio*, that would have been produced in London had Maretzek remained there. See "Max Maretzek," unidentified New York publication, probably fall 1849.

[6] *New York Times*, 10 February 1889, p. 16; Charles Haywood, Introduction to Maretzek's *Revelations of an Opera Manager* (New York: Dover, 1968), xix-xxii.

**Fig. 1.   MAX MARETZEK, lithograph by F. D'Avignon,
from a daguerreotype by Brawley**

Courtesy of the Music Division, New York Public Library for the Performing Arts,
and the Astor, Lenox, and Tilden Foundations

His unemployment was no doubt a consideration in Maretzek's acceptance of an offer from Edward P. Fry (brother of composer, William Henry Fry)
to become music director for the second season of the Astor Place Opera House
in New York in 1848. The opportunity to present opera to audiences of all classes
in a democratic society, a lifelong ambition of Maretzek, offered further incentive.
He arrived in New York in September on the passenger ship *Washington* and,
following a New York gala at which he conducted on October 2, made a
memorable debut in Philadelphia three days later with the Astor Place Company
on tour.

*   *   *   *

But there are some few impossibilities in this world, which cannot be over-come. Amongst these, may be reckoned the attempt to make an elephant execute a pas seul *upon the tight-rope; the endeavor to make a vessel sail in the teeth of a sharp north-easter (the Flying-Dutchman always excepted; or the idea of stopping a cannon-ball when once discharged from the tube that held it, on the application of a match to its priming) with a sheet of blotting paper. All of these are simple impossibilities. But, there is one which is more impossible still. This is the belief that you can make a prima donna sing, when her mind is made up not to do so.*

The house was full; the overture had been played by the orchestra; the tenor had sung his cavatina; and the blonde and bewitching Truffi appears upon the stage. A tremendous reception is awarded to the Norma of the hour, who receives it as a really savage prima donna invariably receives applause, with a tender grace that is truly touching. She sings a few bars of the recitative, staggers, and falls upon the stage, fainting. Druids, call-boys, and Roman soldiers, rush towards her. Oroveso brings a glass of cold water, and Adalgisa applies a smelling-bottle to her nose, but she does not move. Pollio calls on his Italian gods in no very choice Italian; a cockney carpenter vents an oath such as are sworn upon the banks of the Thames, and nine-tenths of the male chorus swear as lustily in German as the lanz-knechts *were wont to do. As for the parquet, it shrieks with laughter; from the boxes breaks a storm of hisses, while the gallery hoots in wrath or yells with delight at the unwonted spectacle. Mr. Fry is about to rend his hair, but thinks better of it as he remembers that he wears a wig. The curtain comes down, and the manager walks before it, announcing that "in consequence of Signora Truffi's sudden (he lays an ugly emphasis upon this word) indisposition, the money (here, I thought I heard him groan) would be returned, or the tickets (in saying this, his face recovered from its previous gloom) might be retained for the next performance."*

So ended the first night of the season in Philadelphia.[7]

*   *   *   *

When the company failed the next spring, Maretzek assumed the position of manager. He subsequently managed a series of New York-based opera companies under varying names (often with overlapping personnel) that toured the eastern United States, Cuba, and Mexico. Although Maretzek's companies performed Italian opera almost exclusively, they offered some seasons of opera

---

[7] *C&Q*, 34-35.

sung in French, German, and English, and also performed French and German operas in Italian—for example, Meyerbeer's *Gli Ugonotti* (*Les Huguenots*) and *La stella del Nord* (*L'étoile du Nord*).

In his first letter in *Crotchets and Quavers* (to Berlioz) Maretzek describes New York as sharing the role of musical capital in the United States with Boston and Philadelphia and notes the strength of French opera in New Orleans, the first city in the U.S. where opera had flourished.[8] While Boston and Philadelphia, as well as other urban centers throughout the country, were important stops for touring opera companies, and New Orleans remained the center for French opera, the majority of American companies were organized in New York and most U.S. premieres took place there. These companies were for the most part a series of transitory troupes that existed for sometimes only a single season and were then quickly reorganized, perhaps with some new singers, and under a slightly different name and new management.

Opera seasons reflected the fragility of the companies that presented them. Between 1863 and 1867, typical of other companies of the era, Maretzek's company had seasons that ranged from sixteen to forty nights of productions. The company averaged twenty-six nights of performances, often broken into two subscription series, frequently followed by a shorter run of six or seven nights featuring a single new production. The subscription series offered a different opera every night, although some operas were repeated, particularly when they were performed for matinees and performances in Brooklyn. A hiatus of several days, sometimes coinciding with a holiday or attributable to some other explanation, often preceded the shorter season to allow time for rehearsal and preparation of the new work. Several benefit performances followed the end of the subscription series and usually preceded the shorter season when there was one. These performances featured the manager or the stars of the company, and the work presented—whether it was in the company's current repertory or not—was one in which the honoree had won renown. Proceeds went to the benefit recipient, although Maretzek sometimes shared returns for his own benefits with his singers.

Regular opera nights in Manhattan were Mondays, Wednesdays, and Fridays. Performances on Thursdays were added in the spring of 1864, but thereafter through 1867 Thursdays were dropped in favor of performances on Tuesdays; there were also Saturday matinees, which were attended almost exclusively by women and visitors from outside Manhattan. Performances at the Brooklyn

---

[8] From Maretzek's letter to Hector Berlioz in Paris, 25 July 1855, in ibid., 33.

Academy of Music were usually on Thursday nights. While the repertory to be performed was announced at a season's outset when subscription sales opened, it frequently fell victim to the vagaries of the time. Operas scheduled might be altered in the midcourse of a season or cancelled altogether because of a singer's indisposition, the weather, a musicians' strike, the response of the public, or for any number of other reasons. Between 1863 and 1867, Maretzek's company traditionally presented the spring and fall seasons at the New York Academy of Music and before, between, and after these, made shorter tours to other eastern cities. Maretzek often spent summers in Europe lining up new talent for his next season. Rapid new steamships facilitated travel during this era and brought a flow of visiting singers from Europe to the U.S.[9]

New York City at this time comprised only Manhattan; the four other boroughs were not consolidated until 1898. With a population of 813,669 in 1860, New York was larger than the next two largest U.S. cities, Philadelphia and Brooklyn, combined. Its streets were laid out on the grid plan that was adopted in 1811 for development above Fourteenth Street; most of the city lay below Forty-second Street. Ladies' Mile was the equivalent of today's Fifth Avenue shopping district and stretched along Broadway and Sixth Avenue, between Ninth and Twenty-third Streets. The Union Square district was a vibrant center for theater, fine dining, and hotels during the 1870s. The first sky-scraper, at seven and a half stories, was the Equitable Life Assurance Building (120 Broadway), designed by George B. Post and completed in 1870, although several ten-story buildings dominated the skyline by mid-decade. The first (experimental) segment of an elevated mass transit line appeared in the late 1860s, but transportation was otherwise by horse-drawn vehicle. Progress through the clogged streets was thus often slow. Belgian blocks (square, granite stones), as well as other materials, such as concrete, wood, macadam, and gravel, were the primary paving staples.[10]

Opera management was highly competitive, although the shifting alliances and partnerships suggest that personal relationships between impresarios may have been less charged than some of the rhetoric might suggest. One of Maretzek's closest competitors was Bernard Ullman (figs. 2 and 3), a nonmusician who emigrated from Hungary to the United States about 1842 and is credited with introducing systematic profit-making techniques to the field of music management, thereby

---

[9] Edwin G. Burrows and Mike Wallace, *Gotham, A History of New York City to 1898* (New York: Oxford University Press, 1999), 724.

[10] *The Encyclopedia of New York City* (New Haven: Yale University Press, 1995), ed. Kenneth Jackson. S.v. "Population," by Nathan Kantrowitz; "Ladies' Mile," by Amanda Aaron; "Skyscrapers, 1870-1916," by Sarah Bradford Landau; "Subways," by Peter Derrick; "Paving," by Craig D. Bida.

Fig. 2.   BERNARD ULLMAN,
photograph by Numa Blanc & Cie

Courtesy of the Bibliothèque Nationale, Paris

Fig. 3.   BERNARD ULLMAN,
photograph by Ch. Reutlinger

Courtesy of the Bibliothèque Nationale, Paris

transforming it from an art form to a commodity.[11] He moved to Paris in 1862, then returned to the U.S. in 1875-76 for a tour, serving as Hans von Bülow's manager.

Maurice Strakosch, born in Gross-Seelowitz (now Zidlochovice, and near Brno), was Maretzek's other major rival (and also his cousin; fig. 4). Strakosch arrived in New York at age twenty-three, earlier in the same year as Maretzek.[12] A virtuoso pianist, he had run away from home at age twelve and had toured Germany extensively as a child. Strakosch made his New York debut as a pianist on 10 June 1848, and he soon after became a member of Maretzek's orchestra for a short time. He was a composer, as well as co-owner of a piano store with Henry C. Watson, who was later the music critic of *The New York Tribune*.[13] Several members of his family were musicians or active in opera management. The mezzo soprano Amalia Patti, whom he subsequently married, was a member of the first concert troupe he organized. He managed and coached the early career of his young sister-in-law, coloratura soprano Adelina Patti, who was later celebrated throughout the United States and Europe. Maretzek's company gave the premiere of Strakosch's only known opera, *Giovanna Prima di Napoli* (January 1851), as well as four subsequent performances of it.[14] By 1856 Strakosch and Ullman had become serious rivals to Maretzek and remained so until both relocated to Europe. In 1861 Strakosch and his family, including Adelina, moved to Europe, where he lived for the remainder of his life.[15] His memoirs, *Souvenirs d'un impresario*, were published in 1887, the year of his death. His younger brother Max, who had no music training and had initially entered the dry-goods business after his arrival in New York at age eighteen in 1853, became his

---

[11] Lawrence Lerner, "The Rise of the Impresario: Bernard Ullman and the Transformation of Musical Culture in Nineteenth Century America" (Ph.D. diss., University of Wisconsin, 1970): 3-4.

[12] It was Strakosch who conveyed Fry's offer to Maretzek in London and described the opportunities for a young artist in the U.S. in glowing terms. See "Max Maretzek," unidentified New York publication, probably fall 1849.

[13] *New York Times*, 11 November 1887, p. 5; Lahee, *Grand Opera in America*, 139; *New York Musical World* 4, no. 1, whole no. 75 (4 September 1852): 11. Strakosch's prize of $24,940 from a winning Maryland lottery ticket (1852) may have contributed to the financing of his piano store; see *New York Times*, 5 October 1852, p. 1.

[14] Katherine K. Preston, *Opera on the Road: Traveling Opera Troupes in the United States, 1825-60* (Urbana: University of Illinois Press, 1993), 174, 185-88.

[15] Max Strakosch later attributed the move to an effort to avoid ruin in New York (*Brooklyn Eagle*, 12 October 1875, p. 2). The Maretzek and Strakosch families apparently remained in contact: the Maretzek file in the Harold Lineback collection, New York Philharmonic Archives, contains two photos (dated 4 May 1869, Paris, and 31 August 1870) of Strakosch's daughter, Julia, one of which is inscribed on the verso, "to my darling cousin Marie" (Maretzek's daughter).

Fig. 4.   MAURICE STRAKOSCH, drawing on stone by F. D'Avignon, from a daguerreotype by P. Haas (New York: William Hall and Son)

Courtesy of the Music Division, New York Public Library for the Performing Arts, and the Astor, Lenox, and Tilden Foundations

agent four years later, when he was in partnership with Ullman.   Max continued to assist Maurice from the U.S. after Maurice's return to Europe; he organized an Italian opera company of his own in 1865.   The two also managed the career of their niece the diva Clara Louise Kellogg, who married Karl Strakosch, their nephew and her manager of many years.   Maurice's son, Robert, later became an impresario in Paris, where Maurice's brother Ferdinand was also an impresario. Robert's cousin Edgar Strakosch, active in the business aspect of grand opera, was a manager of the Baltimore Music Hall and was later associated with Maurice Grau at the Metropolitan Opera of New York.[16]

---

[16] Maurice Strakosch, "Strakosch and Patti," *Musical Courier* 41, no. 17, whole no. 1074 (24 October 1900): 26.

The explanation for the intriguing confluence in New York of the Maretzek family, the Strakosches, and, as will be seen, the Graus, all families of Jewish descent who emigrated in mid-century from Brno (capital of Moravia) to New York, where they became active in artist management, probably begins in Moravia.[17] Restrictions enacted by the Habsburgs in 1726-27 had limited the number of Jewish families permitted to reside in Moravia (also in Bohemia), as well as the number of marriages authorized. These laws were repealed in 1848-49, and the state granted full political emancipation to Jews by 1867. But Maretzek's generation had reached young adulthood earlier. As Czech nationalism took hold, both Germans and Jews were increasingly excluded from Czech life.[18] German language and culture had been pervasive in Czech Jewish communities in the first half of the century, which facilitated young Moravian Jews' emigration to Vienna (the city where Maretzek pursued his university degree), the nearest major city and a most frequent destination.[19] The revolutions throughout Europe in 1848 were no doubt a factor that contributed to the resettlement of many families in North America. A conversation that Maretzek describes with Verdi in his third book indicates that the remuneration for conducting in New York, at least, compared favorably with European rates (see p. 81 below).

Whereas New York had been almost exclusively Protestant through the 1830s, mass migrations of Irish Catholics and German Jews, the latter encouraged by strict economic and social restrictions in various German states, transformed the city during the 1840s and 1850s. By 1855, Catholics were the largest denomination, and Jews numbered 40,000 by 1859. The German Jews blended indistinguishably with other Germans for the most part, and encountered little prejudice, unlike the Irish, who experienced a strong anti-Catholic backlash, whether of the Catholic faith or not.[20]

Maretzek referred to himself as a "good Christian" and professed his faith in God, eschewing a label of Roman Catholic, Episcopalian, Greek Orthodox, Lutheran, or Presbyterian.[21] Although a secular Jew, he was nonetheless occasionally the target of anti-Semitic remarks. Nathaniel Willis, probably drawing his inferences

---

[17] This issue is further explored in my article, "A Confluence of Moravian Impresarios: Max Maretzek, the Strakosches, and the Graus," in *Importing Culture: European Music and Musicians in New York, 1840-1890*, ed. John Graziano (Rochester: University of Rochester Press, 2006), in press.

[18] Sayer, 107.

[19] Hillel J. Kieval, *The Making of Czech Jewry: National Conflict in Bohemia, 1870-1918* (New York: Oxford University Press, 1988), 6-8, 12, 15-16.

[20] Burrows and Wallace, 748-49.

[21] From Maretzek's letter to Fiorentino in Paris, 28 July 1855, in *C&Q*, 69, 101.

Fig. 5.   ASTOR PLACE OPERA HOUSE, New York City, in 1850, lithograph
(New York: Henry Hoff, 1850)

Courtesy of New York Historical Society

from a benefit performance for the Young Men's Hebrew Benevolent Association, wrote in a later review of Mozart's *Don Giovanni*, "our little Hebrews are scarcely to blame for failing when put to work that is altogether beyond them," and he continued on to "pray" for their "banishment" and a "coming of the Gentiles."[22] Madame Maretzek was Catholic, as were their two daughters.[23]

Following a three-week engagement in Philadelphia, Fry's company opened in New York at the Astor Place Opera House on 1 November 1848, with Max Maretzek as conductor. The Astor Place Opera House was situated between Broadway and the Bowery, one side faced Eighth Street, and the other Astor Place (fig. 5). The house was important to New York's musical life for several years; it was one of a number of short-lived theaters that housed opera prior to the creation of the Academy of Music. Astor Place Opera House had opened a year earlier (22 November 1847) with Verdi's *Ernani*. A committee of stockholders governed it; the theater, with 1,800 seats, was, in addition to opera, home to drama, vaudeville, balls, and concerts. Maretzek's term as manager pro tem extended from 19 March 1849 until the season's close on April 12.

---

[22] Vera Brodsky Lawrence, *Strong on Music*, 3 vols. (Chicago: University of Chicago Press, 1995), 2: 9-10. Maretzek describes his response to Willis's attacks in *C&Q*, 83-85.

[23] From Maretzek's chapter 6, "Opera in Mexico," in *Sharps and Flats* [hereafter, *S&F*], 57; the younger daughter left her estate not otherwise designated to St. Patrick's Cathedral, "Last will and testament of Antoinette Maretzek Lindsay," 11 May 1944, N.Y. County (she died 11 May 1952); the elder daughter made a gift in her will to a Catholic Church in Rossville, S.I., "Last will and testament of Marie A. Wilbur," filed in Surrogate Court, County of Richmond, S.I., 9 October 1944 (she died 7 July 1948).

Crotchets and Quavers
1849

Maretzek learned that he was the successful candidate for the position of manager of the Astor Place Opera House the morning following a devastating riot in which twenty-three people were killed and scores more seriously injured. On the night of 10 May 1849 an unruly mob had gathered outside the opera house to protest a performance of *Macbeth* featuring the English actor William C. Macready. The Astor Place Riot was the culmination of a long-simmering feud between partisans of Macready and the American actor Edwin Forrest. At Macready's first appearance in the play, fans of the two actors created a disturbance, and a placard was displayed on stage: "The friends of order will remain quiet." The friends of order were, however, outnumbered. Arrests made inside the house may have triggered an assault outside the house by a crowd of several thousand. A nearby sewer project provided a ready supply of large paving stones that were hurled at the entrances and windows. The military was called in to assist the overwhelmed police force and fired upon the angry mob, killing and injuring bystanders as well as active participants.[24]

Unable to find singers willing to perform in the opera house after that horrendous incident, Maretzek set sail for Europe in July in search of new singers for his fall season. In *Crotchets and Quavers* he deplores the cost of the lease on the opera house and rails against the inadequate funds that were his for hiring singers. He scoffs at a suggestion from his patrons that he engage Giulia Grisi, a prominent Italian soprano then active in Paris and London, and her stage partner and companion, Italian tenor Giovanni Mario, the preeminent Italian bass Luigi Lablache, or Jenny Lind (later procured by P.T. Barnum). Sophie Cruvelli, German soprano, and Raffaele Mirate, Italian tenor, were beyond his means, although within a few years they were to command even higher fees. He congratulates himself on the creditable company he was able to assemble, despite his limited means. It consisted principally of sopranos Apollonia Bertucca (later his wife; fig. 6), Teresa Truffi (apparently recovered from the indisposition she suffered in Philadelphia), and Eufrasia Borghese, tenors Giuseppe Forti and Giuseppe Guidi, and basses Ferdinando Beneventano and Pietro Novelli.[25]

---

[24] *Account of the Terrific and Fatal Riot at the New-York Astor Place Opera House* (New York: Museum of the City of New York, 1999), 20.

[25] Mentioned in Maretzek's letter to Fiorentino in Paris, 28 July 1855, in *C&Q*, 76-79, 82.

Fig. 6.   APOLLONIA BERTUCCA-MARETZEK, lithograph

Courtesy of Harry Ransom Humanities Research Center,
University of Texas at Austin

Maretzek's company opened with Donizetti's *Lucia di Lammermoor* at Astor Place on November 1 to generally favorable reviews. He rationed his new singers at a rate of one per performance, in part as a marketing ploy, but also to camouflage the technical difficulty that not all of them had yet arrived from Europe.[26] Maretzek offended members of his orchestra at the rehearsal preceding the dress rehearsal for the December 10th U.S. premiere of Donizetti's *Maria di Rohan*, and nearly the entire orchestra resigned. Overnight he combed the city for a new orchestra, then rehearsed its members in locked quarters throughout the next day, and began the performance that evening punctually at 8 o'clock.[27] The first season closed on 7 March 1850, with a benefit performance of *Don Giovanni* for Maretzek; he had ended the season with artistic success, but some $3,600 in debt.[28]

1850

As his future in New York became more secure, Maretzek brought his family to New York from Moravia. His brother Albert, former stage manager at Drury Lane, assisted with opera management, and his younger brother Raphael, with business aspects.[29] In the early 1850s, his parents, Raphael and Anna, lived with his sisters, Rosa and Leontine, at 94 East Tenth Street, next door to tenor Salvatore Patti (the first manager of Astor Place) and his wife, soprano Caterina Barili Patti, and their three daughters, Amalia, Carlotta, Adelina, and son, Carlo.[30] Both Salvatore and Amalia were members of Maretzek's Astor Place Company from 1849 through 1852.[31] The Maretzek sisters were schoolmates and playmates

---

[26] Lawrence, 1:581.

[27] Letter to Fiorentino, 28 July 1855, in *C&Q*, 88-90.

[28] Lawrence, 2:11-12.

[29] Ibid., 2:592n. Albert briefly ran a liquor store in the second block north of Canal Street at 456 ½ Broadway (Doggett/Rode 1851-52 New York City directory).

[30] The Maretzeks lived at 168 E. Tenth Street and the Pattis at 170. By 1890, when *Sharps and Flats* was published, the houses had been renumbered to 94 and 96. These houses, as well as number 90, have now been demolished, and a residential building, with retail shops facing Third Ave., extends from E. Tenth to E. Ninth Street. The Pattis moved to the Bronx in 1855. At about the same time, the Maretzeks moved to a series of addresses on Ninth Ave. (200, 198, 202). Albert Maretzek and Maurice Strakosch are also listed at the 202 address in 1857. A few years later the Maretzeks moved to Sixth Ave. and then to E. Thirty-second Street in 1861, the final listing in New York City directories.

[31] *New York Times*, 15 December 1915, p. 15.

of the two younger Patti daughters. Maretzek recalls Adelina Patti's after-school visits with his sister to his office, when she would astonish them with her uncanny ability to sing any aria or song requested in her lovely pure soprano voice.[32] Two of Maretzek's sisters later married leading singers in his company.[33]

Apollonia (Nell) Bertucca [Bertucat] and Maretzek were married in 1851.[34] She was born in the French village of Les Grand Veaux (near Vichy).[35] After demonstrating an early talent for the harp, she began lessons with a local flautist. She attended the Paris Conservatoire, then studied harp with Théodore Labarre and composition with Friedrich von Flotow, the composer of *Martha*. At age thirteen Apollonia Bertucca was accompanied in concert by Franz Liszt. She played before Queen Victoria and Prince Albert at age fourteen and was presented with turquoise earrings, a brooch, and bracelets.[36] One of her pupils was Lady Ada Lovelace, daughter of Lord Byron. By 1841 Bertucca was a prominent harpist in London. Nevertheless, one evening she substituted as a singer for an absent soprano. With the encouragement of Giovanni Battista Rubini, who heard her performance, she began vocal studies, traveling to Milan to study with Giacomo Panizza, chief conductor at La Scala. She made her debut as Amina in Bellini's *La sonnambula* at the Teatro S Benedetto, Venice, in 1843. She then studied with Rossini and toured Europe, appearing under the management of

---

[32] Chapter 6, "Opera in Mexico," in *S&F*, 49.

[33] Rosa married Ignazio Marini on 20 September 1851 (*Brooklyn Eagle*, 22 September 1851, p. 2). A son of Marini's, probably by his first wife, soprano Antoinetta Marini-Rainieri, sang (baritone) with Maretzek's company in 1857 (*Brooklyn Eagle*, 28 October 1857, p. 3). Maretzek describes Marini as "frequently ill-humored," "capricious," and "strangely peevish and splenetic" in *C&Q*, 169.

Sophie married Geremia Bettini, on 27 April 1852 (*New York Tribune*, 23 April 1852, p. 6); they had three children by 1857 (*Brooklyn Eagle*, 28 October 1857, p. 3). Maretzek recounts his efforts in *Crotchets and Quavers* to curb the young Bettini's exploits by placing him under surveillance (167-69). Bettini died in Italy at age forty-two: *La Revue et Gazette musicale de Paris* 32 (16 April 1865): 127.

[34] *Richmond County Advance*, 23 January 1909 (obituary).

[35] Her father was a descendant of one of Lafayette's staff in the American Revolution and was awarded 20,510 acres in Kentucky by the U.S. Government as an expression of gratitude. Madame Maretzek initiated legal proceedings in 1882 to reclaim the land. Letter to Madame from J.M. Bent, 22 May 1882, and clipping from an unidentified source, both in the private collection of George Del Grosso, New York City.

[36] Mme Maretzek's harp is now in the collection at Historic Richmond Town (441 Clarke Ave., Staten Island). A sympathetic stagehand once concealed the harp from creditors in the stage rafters, only revealing his subterfuge to the despairing impresario and his wife the next morning. *New York Times*, 15 September 1901, p. SM5.

Maurice Strakosch in Turin. In an interview she later recalled that Maretzek had sought her out in Paris and offered her the engagement for his first season at Astor Place.[37] Apollonia Bertucca made her U.S. debut as Desdemona in Rossini's *Otello* in November 1849.

Lillian Nordica [Norton], the American soprano, was probably Mme Maretzek's best-known pupil. They met in April 1876 when Nordica auditioned in Boston for German dramatic soprano Therese Tietjens.[38] Madame Maretzek was at the time performing as a harpist with the Tietjens Company, which had been touring the U.S. The audition took place in Tietjens's dressing room following a performance. Mme Maretzek offered to coach Nordica in the operatic repertoire at no charge if she came to New York that summer, an offer that Nordica accepted. She took three lessons a week, sometimes boarding the ferry to Staten Island for a lesson at the Maretzeks' home. Madame took her pupil to meet tenor Pasquale Brignoli and was instrumental in finding engagements for her. Nordica continued her studies into the fall. Ira Glackens, Nordica's biographer, describes an affectionate reunion of the two in Chicago in 1889. Nordica later attributed the success of her performance as Giaconda at the opening of the 1905-06 season at the Met to a visit she paid to Mme Maretzek the preceding day at her home on Staten Island.[39]

Mme Maretzek, who conducted the family's real estate transactions, purchased their home on Staten Island in July 1853 from a local physician James O. Van Hoevenberg. The family was to reside there for nearly fifty years. The house, on Bloomingdale Road in Pleasant Plains, is located on a hill overlooking New York Bay. It still stands, although it has been moved slightly from its original site on twenty-seven acres, and trees obscure the harbor view.[40] The drive leading

---

[37] Ida Howard, "A Prima Donna of the Old Days: Madame Maretzek's Reminiscences of the Opera Stage," *San Francisco Chronicle*, 1 February 1903, p. 8.

[38] Mme Tietjens had arrived in the U.S. in September 1875 with Maretzek, and he arranged and conducted her opera season at the Academy of Music in January and February 1876. *Brooklyn Eagle*, 21 September 1875, p. 4; George Odell, *Annals of the New York Stage*, 15 vols. (New York: Columbia University Press, 1927-49), 10:69.

[39] Ira Glackens, *Yankee Diva: Lillian Nordica and the Golden Days of Opera* (New York: Coleridge, 1963), 26-31, 145-46, 225.

[40] Richmond County Real Estate Records: Deeds, liber 19, p. 3. Prior to purchasing the house in Pleasant Plains, Maretzek had lived briefly in Manhattan at 113 Liberty (later part of the site occupied by the World Trade Center), at 111 Clinton Place, and rented a summerhouse in Rosebank, Staten Island, in 1850. Since he did not need the house the following winter, Maretzek offered it to Antonio Meucci, former superintendent of mechanics at Havana's Tacon Theater, and his wife, former head wardrobe mistress, when they chose to remain in the U.S. after visiting with the Havana Opera

to the house is now a street named for Maretzek. The Maretzeks often held open house for friends, neighbors, and business associates on their lawn on Sundays.[41] Maretzek's horse and buggy were a familiar sight to the island's south shore residents as he made his daily trips to Clifton to board the ferry for Manhattan.[42] In addition to Marie, born in 1850 and the custodian of her father's unpublished manuscript, the Maretzeks had a second daughter, Antoinette, born in 1860, who would have been the baby Maretzek mentions in *Sharps and Flats* and for whom his wife pleaded with Mexican women allied with bandits on their second Mexican tour (1861) for restitution of the baby's underwear.[43] Both daughters and a son, Max Jr. (b. 1853), were musicians, and their father often accompanied them at the piano as they were growing up.[44]

The Maretzeks' choice of Staten Island may have been influenced by the existence there of a Moravian community. Early members of the Protestant denomination, the Unitas Fratrum (United Brethren, or Moravian Church, a sect popularly referred to as "the Moravians"), had fled oppression in Moravia, Bohemia, and Poland in the late 1720s, and subsequently had established missionary colonies in many countries, including the United States.[45] Staten Island, with its inviting expanse of unsettled territory, attracted a number of small religious groups. In the early eighteenth century the United Brethren had settled in New Dorp. Among the converts were early members of the Vanderbilt family, who

---

Company. Natives of Florence, the Meuccis had spent fifteen years in Havana. Lorenzo Salvi, tenor with the Havana Company, lived in the Staten Island house with them briefly, as did Giuseppe Garibaldi, the Italian patriot who helped unify Italy. Meucci, an inventor, also ran a candle-making factory that employed the occupants of the household and other local Italian immigrants. Garibaldi returned to Italy in 1854, and Meucci lived on in the house until his death in 1889.

In 2002, the U.S. Congress passed Resolution 269, recognizing Meucci as the true inventor of the telephone. The Gothic Revival frame house (moved approximately 400 yards from its original site) is now the Garibaldi Meucci Museum (420 Tomkins Ave., Rosebank, S.I); *S&F*, 10-11; http://www.garibaldimeuccimuseum.org.

[41] Years later, another harpist, Maude Morgan (managed at one time by Maurice Strakosch), lived in a converted icehouse alongside a pond on the former Maretzek property. Mabel Abbott, "Musical Traditions in Old Homes," *New York Sun*, 28 September 1929, p. 24.

[42] Anita Kershaw Jacobsen, "Max Maretzek, Staten Islander," *The Staten Island Historian* 5, no. 3 (July-September 1942): 17. The Staten Island railroad (Clifton to Tottenville) was completed in 1860, and the municipal ferry to Manhattan began service in 1890.

[43] *S&F*, 56-57.

[44] Jacobsen, 23.

[45] *The Encyclopedia of Religion* (New York: Macmillan, 1986-87), 10:107. S.v. "Moravians," by David A. Schattschneider.

had been a part of the Dutch colony. A meeting house constructed in 1763 was burned by the British during the Revolution, but a Moravian church, at the entrance to the Moravian Cemetery, which contains the Maretzek family burial plots, still stands in New Dorp.[46] Many German immigrants, refugees from the political upheaval in Europe, settled there around 1848.[47]

The month following the close of the Astor Place season, the wealthy businessman and impresario Francisco Martí y Torrens returned to New York with his acclaimed Havana Opera Company for their first visit since 1847. They opened with Bellini's *Norma* on 11 April 1850. The theater, Niblo's, was located in an entertainment complex at Broadway and Prince Streets. It had opened in 1829 on the site of a popular outdoor summer garden. The facility had been destroyed by fire in 1846 and rebuilt in 1849. The company's visit took the city by storm. Their final performance of *Lucia di Lammermoor* on May 8 attracted an audience of approximately 3,500, the largest yet for opera in New York. The company traveled to Boston, where they met with similar praise, and returned to the Astor Place Opera House, June 3-July 1. They appeared July 8-September 7 at Castle Garden, another popular summer garden theater, which had originally been built as a fort during the War of 1812. Castle Garden was located on an artificial island off the Battery and linked to Manhattan by causeway, and was soon to become the site of Jenny Lind's U.S. debut. The Havana company continued to draw extraordinary crowds at Castle Garden—and at a reduced admission price of fifty cents per person.[48]

The Havana Opera Company had no sooner departed from New York when Swedish soprano Jenny Lind arrived there. The excitement generated by the Havana company soared to new heights in anticipation of Lind's visit, fueled by a shrewd publicity blitz masterminded by her manager, the formidable Phineas T. Barnum. With his second season scheduled to begin in scarcely a month, the intense pressure from such stellar attractions cast Maretzek into despair. In his letter to bass Luigi Lablache in *Crochets & Quavers*, he ruefully laments his lot: "Figure to yourself the position of a luckless impresario with a company of Truffis and Beneventanos upon his hands, and the lease of the Astor Place Opera House upon his shoulders, with Jenny Lind and Barnum, real genius and undoubted 'humbug' in a strange co-partnership, starring ominously in his face." Maretzek's solution was "to enter upon the contest, with the 'Prince of Humbugs'

---

[46] Wheaton J. Lane, *Commodore Vanderbilt: An Epic of the Steam Age* (New York: Alfred Knopf, 1942), 6-7.

[47] Dorothy Valentine Smith, *Staten Island, Gateway to New York* (Philadelphia: Chilton, 1970), 153.

[48] Lawrence, 2:16-17, 27, 33, 47.

using his own weapons."[49] He had already assembled a well-rounded company of singers and a respectable chorus and orchestra, but a summer recruiting trip by his brother Albert and tenor Giuseppe Forti had failed to produce fresh, unknown talent.[50] His weapon of choice was Teresa Parodi, Italian soprano (pupil of Giuditta Pasta), who had made her London debut in 1849 and whom Benjamin Lumley was willing to release from a contract with Her Majesty's Company.

Upon securing funds to underwrite Parodi's engagement, Maretzek set to work manufacturing puffs, commendatory letters, and articles à la Barnum. His efforts came to no avail, however, in the onslaught of the Barnum "Niagara." Finally, in desperation, he planted a rumor romantically linking the young, attractive Parodi with the sexagenarian Duke of Devonshire. The rumor caught fire and spread nationwide within a few weeks. Maretzek's response was to decline comment, quietly open his subscription list, and begin his season without announcing the names of the artists. Audiences were sparse at the season's opening on 21 October 1850 but, with Parodi's arrival, Maretzek immediately cancelled all further subscription sales and doubled the price of admission. Parodi made her U.S. debut as Norma (her mentor Pasta had created the title role) on November 4 and played to full houses night after night. Maretzek drew his New York season, as well as ambitious simultaneous seasons in Philadelphia and Baltimore, to a "triumphant" close in mid-February.[51]

1851

Having met the challenge of Lind with Parodi, Maretzek's response to the threat posed by the Havana Opera Company, then managed by Don Francisco Martí, was to lure away its leading singers when their contracts expired. He succeeded in this maneuver by positioning his troupe in Charleston when the Havana singers, en route from Havana back to Europe, stopped in Charleston after their contracts' expiration.[52] In June he returned victoriously to New York (following appearances from mid-February through May in Boston, Charleston, and Augusta, Georgia) with his expanded company, which now comprised his former Astor Place singers

---

[49] Teresa Truffi and Sesto Benedetti had recently married. Lawrence, 2:97; *C&Q*, 122-23.

[50] Preston, *Opera*, 160-61.

[51] From Maretzek's letter to Luigi LaBlache, 28 August 1855, in *C&Q*, 124-27; see also Preston, *Opera*, 174, 191-92.

[52] Preston, *Opera*, 206-08.

(minus Parodi, who had left the troupe at the conclusion of the Boston engagement), fortified by the Havana troupe.[53] The company included prima donnas Balbina Steffanone and Angelina Bosio, contralto Carolina Vietti, tenors Geremia Bettini and Domenico Lorini, baritone Cesare Badiali, and basses Ignazio Marini and Domenico Coletti. Luigi Arditi shared conducting responsibilities with Maretzek.[54] Maretzek later described the company as "the very best which has ever been put together upon this side of the Atlantic."[55] While leading singers of this caliber were not unusual, an entire company of such magnificence was extraordinary. The memory of the Havana company's success at Castle Garden the preceding summer remained vivid; the possibility of offering opera at affordable prices to a broader stratum of society seemed within reach.

Maretzek's company began a short season on June 3 at Astor Place, preceding their opening at Castle Garden on June 16. The success of the previous summer, however, was not to be repeated. Maretzek laments that some nights drew as few as 100 to 150 spectators in a theater with a seating capacity of 5,000.[56] By season's end on September 19, Maretzek put his losses at $22,000. To make matters worse, the artists, liberated from rigid regimes in Italy and Havana and savoring their newfound independence in New York, proved an unwieldy lot to govern.[57]

At season's close, Maretzek dispatched one part of his company on an ill-fated tour to Richmond, Charleston, and Savannah through the end of December and took the rest of the company to Philadelphia. He reopened at Astor Place on 3 November 1851 featuring a repertory similar to the summer's at Castle Garden. This season was much more successful, however, attracting larger audiences and garnering critical acclaim. The season closed on December 20, the last time this superb company was to appear intact.[58]

The contingent of his company that had traveled south encountered serious difficulties. Reports reached Maretzek that the agent in charge had antagonized the press in Richmond.[59] From Charleston emerged reports of major personnel battles with the singers. Then the agent reappeared back in New York, having

---

[53] For repertory, see ibid., 195-96.

[54] Arditi, in reviewing the principal impresarios under whom he conducted, ranks Maretzek as the most clever; see Luigi Arditi, *My Reminiscenses* (New York: Da Capo, 1977), 282.

[55] In his letter to Joseph Fischhof in Vienna, August 1855, in *C&Q*, 170.

[56] Lahee, *Grand Opera in America*, 105.

[57] *C&Q*, 158-72.

[58] Lawrence, 2:169, 173, 176.

[59] Preston identifies the agent as Bernard Ullman in *Opera*, 342, note 13b.

abandoned the company in Savannah. Maretzek observed of his company: "Like a blind worm, an oyster, or a polypus, it rejoiced in having neither head nor tail." Maretzek summoned what collateral he could to bring "the headless and tailless company who were amusing themselves as best they could in the city of Savannah" back to New York.[60] He had intended to join the two branches of his company in New Orleans and take the reunited company on to Havana.[61]

1852

Personal antagonisms continued to fester, however, and, as a result, perhaps with encouragement from the aggrieved Don Francisco Martí and William Niblo, whose opera house stood empty, a branch of Maretzek's company broke away in January. The company, calling itself the "Artists' Union Italian Opera Company," offered a competing season, opening with *Norma* at Niblo's Theatre on January 14. The new company included Angiolina Bosio, Rose De Vries, Geremia Bettini (who was to become Maretzek's brother-in-law later in the spring), Domenico Lorini, Cesare Badiali, Domenico Coletti, and conductor Luigi Arditi. Remaining with Maretzek were Balbina Steffanone, Lorenzo Salvi, Federico Beneventano, and Ignazio Marini; Maretzek was also able to persuade Teresa Parodi to return to his company. He postponed the tour to New Orleans, in deference to the wishes of his remaining company and the proprietors of Astor Place, who hoped to forestall the competition.

He opened his season at Astor Place on 19 January 1852 with Donizetti's *La favorita*. The two companies appeared on the same evenings (Mondays, Wednesdays, Fridays, Saturdays), sometimes offering the same opera.[62] No sooner had Maretzek's company opened than the Artists' Union Italian Opera Company reduced admission from one dollar to fifty cents. Maretzek followed suit, reducing admission to fifty cents for the parquet and boxes and twenty-five cents for the amphitheater, with free use of opera glasses accompanying each pair of tickets. A highly-publicized revival by Maretzek's company of Meyerbeer's *Roberto il diavolo* took a loss, despite packed houses. The Artists' Union cut short their season at the escalating competition and, after a performance of Donizetti's *Maria di Rohan* on February 13, fled to Boston, where the company dissolved some three weeks later. A badly-bruised Maretzek then ended his

[60] From Maretzek's letter to M. W. Balfe in Italy, 5 September 1855, in *C&Q*, 197-200, 203.

[61] Preston, *Opera*, 342, note 13b.

[62] Lawrence, 2: 231.

season. But it was a shallow victory, coming so soon after the losses of the summer Castle Garden season: "the defeat had ruined the victor."[63] The Astor Place Opera House also suffered a fatal blow and never again reopened its doors for opera, although it was leased for other purposes, until its sale to the Mercantile Library Association in 1854 and the installation there of the Clinton Hall Library. The building had served as an opera house for a mere five years. It existed for another thirty-six years as Clinton Hall and was finally demolished in 1890.[64]

The illusion haunted both factions of Maretzek's ailing company that Martí would return and take them on tour to New Orleans, Mexico City, and Havana. Maretzek resolved to execute this plan himself with his remaining troupe, in the hope that he might restore his fortunes in the fertile, uncultivated soil for opera in Mexico City—and to preclude any similar tour under contemplation by the Artists' Union. He offered his singers sixty percent raises over their New York contracts, with the stipulation that performances to defray expenses would take place en route. He dispatched an agent to Mexico City to lease the opera house, and the artists traveled by the Ohio and Mississippi rivers under the charge of his brother Albert. Maretzek and his wife traveled via Charleston and Mobile. All arrived safely in New Orleans, although the company had already been obliged to offer two concerts to sustain their lavish expenditures. Free from the threat of rivalry with their colleagues, they proceeded to enjoy the city "as if all the silver mines in Mexico had already been the property of their manager." The troupe, with accompanying persons, had, furthermore, grown from eighteen to twenty-seven, excluding lap dogs and parrots.[65] The company presented a season in New Orleans, 31 March-19 April 1852.[66]

Maretzek, to his own wonder, was able to secure a loan from a local banker and chartered the brig *America* for passage to Veracruz. He confesses to drawing a malicious satisfaction from the discomforts of his spendthrift company in the early days of the seven-day voyage, until he himself was also overcome by seasickness. The population of Veracruz had dwindled from nearly 18,000 in 1803 to approximately 8,000 by 1852. It was hot, the city was dirty, and surrounding swamps harbored mosquitoes that carried malaria and yellow fever.

---

[63] Robert A. Gerson, *Music in Philadelphia* (Westport, CT: Greenwood, 1970), 328-29; *C&Q*, 204-5, 213.

[64] Richard Moody, *The Astor Place Riot* (Bloomington: Indiana University Press, 1958), 220. The building now on this site (21 Astor Place) is being converted to a luxury condominium.

[65] As mentioned in Maretzek's letter to Frederick Gye, manager of the Royal Italian Opera, Covent Garden, London, 18 September 1855, in *C&Q*, 221-24.

[66] Preston, *Opera*, 334.

Blackbirds hovering overhead comprised the city's sole garbage system.[67] At their arrival, Maretzek acceded to the popular demand he had hoped would develop for a concert and was able to delay payment to the captain of the vessel until profits were in hand. This debt had scarcely been dispatched, however, when he learned that stagecoaches to Mexico City, at $60 per person, would cost more than six times the amount he had anticipated and more than the entire trip from New York to Veracruz. He had forgotten that no railroad existed.[68]

Following Mexico's independence from Spain in 1821, development of the Mexican economy (other than in mining) had been severely hampered for some fifty years by lack of a transportation system. Only three highways existed, and all were in a state of severe disrepair. A road from Mexico City to Puebla had been constructed during the late colonial period; failure to reach agreement on a route between Puebla and Veracruz on the coast, however, resulted in three roads for that portion. Tolls were levied for their maintenance, but the roads had deteriorated by 1850, and the tolls were diverted for other purposes. Further road construction was deterred by exorbitant fees demanded by landowners, excessive prices for rock, and hacienda owners who allowed their cattle free range of construction areas. Not until 1865 did a basic network of roads exist between major cities. Before this, stagecoach travel, while disagreeable in any part of the world, was particularly hazardous in Mexico because of lawlessness and the treacherous terrain. Averaging about ten miles an hour, or 110 miles per day, conveyances were also in danger of overturning or becoming stuck in mud. Robberies were common, and not unusual were escorts by hired gunmen, often in league with road agents, who appropriated goods from travelers at will. Stagecoach travel was expensive because the lines were a monopoly.

The bankruptcy of the government had hindered railroad construction, for which foreign sponsorship was deterred by the country's political instability. A railroad under a contract awarded in 1837 to be built between Veracruz and Mexico City failed to materialize. Another contract in 1842 was cancelled seven years later after only three miles of construction. The state of Veracruz had added an additional five miles by 1850. Fifteen miles of serviceable track existed in the entire country by 1860 (in comparison with over 30,000 miles in the U.S.). The poor transportation was detrimental to the country's agriculture (corn and cotton were the chief crops), as well as its commerce.[69]

---

[67] Michael C. Meyer, *The Course of Mexican History* (New York: Oxford University Press, 1991), 362, 393.

[68] *C&Q*, 225-34.

[69] Charles C. Cumberland, *Mexico, the Struggle for Modernity* (London: Oxford University Press, 1968), 155-59, 162-63.

By mid-century, Mexico City was the undisputed center of the country, with a population of 170,000. It boasted clean, wide, bustling streets, filled with expensive, imported carriages, and was better lit than either New York or Philadelphia.[70] During the 1830s, opera sung in Italian became popular and remained the "consuming passion" in musical taste for the duration of the century. Both the aristocracy and the working classes liked music, and a number of Mexicans composed operas based on Italian models. The Teatro Principal, refurbished in 1831, began regular seasons of Italian opera, in which Rossini was a particular favorite.[71]

Maretzek was able to secure postponement of the full amount due for stage-coach travel until his company reached Mexico City, where he arrived with much trepidation. Repayment of the $1,000 loan to the New Orleans banker, the $1,320 still outstanding for the stagecoach, and $2,400 for a month's rent for the Gran Teatro di Santa Anna all fell due on the day the box office opened. Ticket sales on a typical opening day in New York would have fallen short of even $4,000, let alone the $4,720 needed. On the fateful day, he left management of the box office to his brother Albert and, with visions of being thrown into detention by his creditors, went off to pass the time at Chapultepec Park. When he returned, his impassive brother directed a procession of porters, who deposited bags of silver at his feet, one by one, until they numbered seventeen. The proceeds for only twelve nights totaled $18,000.[72]

The season began with *Lucia di Lammermoor* on May 16 and was the highlight of the Mexico City music season. Steffanone, Bertucca, and Salvi were popular members of the notable company. Repertory new to Mexico City included Mozart's *Don Giovanni*,[73] Meyerbeer's *Roberto il diavolo*, Verdi's *I Lombardi alla prima crociata*, and *La favorita, Maria di Rohan, Linda di Chamounix*, and *Don Pasquale*, by Donizetti. Also performed were Donizetti's *Lucrezia Borgia, Parisina, L'elisir d'amore*; Bellini's *Norma, Puritani, Sonnambula*; Rossini's *Barbiere di Siviglia, Otello*; and Verdi's *Ernani*, among other works. The company performed a prospective Mexican national anthem on July 26, composed by Maretzek in honor of President Mariano Arista, who had been elected the previous year. They had planned to offer three subscription series

---

[70] Meyer, 361-62.

[71] Robert Stevenson, *Music in Mexico, A Historical Survey* (New York: Thomas Y. Crowell, 1952), 192-93, 218.

[72] *C&Q*, 237, 247, 267.

[73] *Dwight's Journal of Music* reports a local petition to substitute *Leonora*, by Mexican composer Luis Baca, for *Don Giovanni*, "the uninteresting opera written by 'one Mozart,'" 1 (28 August 1852): 167.

of one month each, but presented a second season of two months beginning in September, followed by a series of benefits, finally closing their very successful season on January 12.[74]

Sharps and Flats
1853

Amid indications of increasing government instability, the company hastily left Mexico City after the abdication of President Arista. Maretzek booked two stage-coaches for their return to Veracruz, via Puebla. With a population of more than 70,000, Puebla was Mexico's second largest city.[75] It had been an important center for music from the sixteenth through the nineteenth centuries, but, after severe political turmoil, by the latter nineteenth century it was in decline.[76] Maretzek likened the company's appearance to a band of Mexican bandits as they prepared to board, for all were heavily armed; he speculated that allies were at greater peril than the enemy had bandits actually been encountered. The company staged a concert in Puebla, which was so poorly attended that Maretzek forwarded all costumes, settings, and music on to Veracruz, except the music for *Don Pasquale*. That opera was well received, and a repeat performance followed the next day. To placate unruly demands, Maretzek scheduled a performance of *Norma*, but he and his troupe made a stealthy 3 o'clock departure from the city early the next morning. They gave several performances in Veracruz, with a

---

[74] Enrique de Olavarria y Ferrari, *Reseña histórica del teatro en México, 1538-1911*, 5 vols. (México: Editorial Porrúa, 1961), 1:512-13, 519, 527; *New York Times*, 11 October 1852, p. 3. Maretzek makes racist comments in describing a Mexican musician: "In spite of his color (for he was a mulatto), he was an excellent violinist, and a tolerably good leader." He then pretends to mistake him for white to flatter him to accept a lower payment for his orchestra. Unable to find white musicians later in Veracruz, he says: "All that I could find were twelve jetty black ones," and repeatedly makes reference to their skin tone in criticizing their playing; see *C&Q*, 240-41, 292-95. Maretzek's remarks were likely reflective of the prevailing attitude toward African Mexican musicians of his time. For example, in Cuba by 1830 one in three professional musicians in Havana were black, soloists were white foreigners, and Cubans had little regard for their own music, and even less for its black performers; see Libby Antarsh Rubin, "Gottschalk in Cuba" (Ph.D. diss., Columbia University, 1974), 27-28.

[75] Meyer, 362.

[76] *The New Grove Dictionary of Music and Musicians* (2001), s.v. "Puebla de los Angeles," by Alice Ray Catalyne.

makeshift orchestra and a fortified chorus bolstered by soloists from the company. Maretzek booked passage to New York for his company on the steamer *Albatross* and for himself and his wife on the *Black Warrior* via New Orleans, Havana, and Mobile. A fierce gale assaulted the Maretzeks' steamer off the Florida coast.[77]

Despite the absence of Maretzek and his company and the closing of the Astor Place Opera House, Italian opera had not disappeared from New York during his year's absence. Jenny Lind had left the U.S. in May 1852. Scarcely a week later, the Italian contralto Marietta Alboni arrived in New York, followed in early September by German soprano Henriette Sontag. Sontag had created the title role in Weber's *Euryanthe* in her early career and had performed the soprano roles in the premieres of Beethoven's Ninth Symphony and his *Missa solemnis*, but she had become the wife of a Sardinian count, and for twenty years had been retired from opera. Alboni, at age thirty, some twenty years younger than Sontag, had studied with Rossini. Her sumptuous voice, together with an unusual range and exceptional technique, was greatly admired. She was one of Walt Whitman's favorite singers.[78] Both singers brought accompanying singers with their entourages and toured to other U.S. cities, as well as giving concerts in New York. By January 1853 both had formed opera companies whose seasons in New York coincided, Alboni at the Broadway Theatre, and Sontag at Niblo's Theatre. In a rivalry reminiscent of the split that had occurred in the Maretzek company barely a year earlier, both companies offered similar repertory on the same nights (Mondays, Wednesdays, and Fridays), and both prima donnas frequently sang the same roles, despite Alboni's lower voice range.[79] To compensate for the scarcity of leading contralto roles, she (and her contemporaries) appropriated soprano roles, albeit usually in transposition.[80]

Maretzek received news of this turn of events while in Veracruz. The two companies now occupied the territory he had vacated. His arrival with yet a third company would, he knew, spell disaster for all three. But his company offered the strong ensemble singers that the other two companies, excelling in prima donnas, lacked. He accordingly resolved to unite his forces with one of the companies, and, as it turned out, eventually with both companies.[81] Maretzek

---

[77] *C&Q*, 275-77, 284-88, 296, 298; *New York Times*, 24 February 1853, p. 1.

[78] Henry Pleasants, *The Great Singers* (New York: Simon & Schuster, 1966), 223; Robert D. Faner, *Walt Whitman & Opera* (Philadelphia: University of Pennsylvania Press, 1951), 59.

[79] Lawrence, 2:323-24.

[80] Pleasants, 224.

[81] *C&Q*, 297, 307; *S&F*, 8-9.

conducted the Alboni Company in Philadelphia in late February-early March. The merged forces of Alboni and Maretzek were renamed the Grand Combination Opera Company, and opened a new season with *Don Pasquale* at Niblo's on March 28. Le Grand Smith, Alboni's manager, continued in the same position, and Maretzek served as artistic director, sharing some conducting duties with Luigi Arditi. An otherwise splendid season was marred by a weeklong indisposition of star tenor Lorenzo Salvi (from Maretzek's company) and ground to an abrupt halt in early May, amid rumors that the agent Ullman had lured away the temperamental Salvi with a much larger salary.

Alboni left the U.S. in early June, and Maretzek then united forces with Sontag (who had been on tour in Philadelphia and Boston when he had merged with Alboni's company) for a summer season at Castle Garden beginning July 11.[82] Visitors to the Crystal Palace Exhibition of Industry of All Nations, built in Bryant Park on the model of London's Crystal Palace and housing the first world's fair to be held in the U.S., were also attracted to the opera. A dollar's admission charge to Castle Garden proved viable, and the season was successful. It closed on August 23 with a benefit for Maretzek.[83] Sontag did not reappear with Maretzek's company, perhaps because of difficulty with her agent, Ullman. Indeed, she appeared only twice more in New York before leaving on tour. Her life was cut tragically short when she and several members of her company died of cholera en route from Mexico City to Veracruz the following year.

Relieved of the threat of rival companies, Maretzek opened his fall season at Niblo's on September 19 with Bellini's *I puritani*. A somewhat faded repertory was enlivened by triumphant new productions of Auber's *La muette de Portici* (as *Masaniello*, in its first New York production in Italian) and Meyerbeer's *Le prophète* (a U.S. premiere, and also sung in Italian). The cost of the Meyerbeer production, which included roller-skating and electric lights (Maretzek observed that the public seemed more enchanted by these than the music), together with the low cost of admission ($1.00), resulted in his failure to meet expenses. A gala benefit for Maretzek planned for the close of the season on December 19 had to be cancelled because of further machinations by tenor Lorenzo Salvi. When Maretzek refused to accede to his demand for advance payment, Salvi failed to appear, signaling the onset of a mutiny: the entire company left on their own for Mexico and Havana, leaving Maretzek alone in New York without a company.[84]

---

[82] *Dwight's Journal of Music* reprints a humorous description from the New Orleans *Picayune* of a rehearsal during this season, 3 (10 September 1853): 181.

[83] Lawrence, 2:337-38, 340-41, 344-46, 348, 351-52.

[84] Ibid., 2:355-56.

1854

Mexico City was blessed by the arrival of two touring opera companies that spring; both the former Maretzek troupe and Sontag's company opened within days of one another in late April at competing theaters. The enthusiasm of the public was soon overshadowed, however, by the deadly cholera epidemic that was to claim Sontag as its first victim on June 17. Several other artists eventually perished as well, and Ignazio Marini narrowly escaped death. The two companies eventually joined forces, presenting their last performance on October 24, before leaving for Europe, via Veracruz, where they presented two performances.[85] It was during this visit that Balbina Steffanone sang the premiere of the Mexican national anthem, with music by Jaime Nuno, in the Gran Teatro de Santa Anna (September 15).

Meanwhile, in New York a new opera house, which was to become the Academy of Music, was under construction on the northeast corner of Fourteenth Street and Irving Place (Union Square). The lavish 25,000 square-foot brick house had a seating capacity of 4,600 (the current Met seats 3,788) and boasted the largest stage in the world. The interior was white and gold, with red velvet seats and gaslight illumination (figs. 7 and 8). Maretzek was in Havana in January, but soon after, trusting that his negotiations in progress for the Academy lease would be successful, he left for Europe to assemble a new company.[86] Negotiations continued at long distance, and Maretzek was promised the contract in May.[87] He returned with his new company in early June and opened at Castle Garden with Donizetti's *Lucia di Lammermoor* on June 30. He presented the U.S. premiere of Verdi's *Luisa Miller* on July 20.

Maretzek's publicity emphasized the ensemble strength of his new company, but its lack of star power was undeniable. The lackluster company was received indifferently by its public. Both Maretzeks contracted cholera, furthermore, as did several other members of the company. Threatening a weak season even

---

[85] Olavarria y Ferrari, 1:571-72, 575-76. Nuno was active in Havana, Mexico, New York, and Buffalo. His submission was the winning entry in a contest organized by President Santa Anna for a musical setting to a text by Francisco González Bocanegra, written in November 1853. Giovanni Bottesini conducted the premiere. Nuno later conducted for the Maretzek company's 1862 visit to Havana and shared the conductor's podium with Maretzek for Maretzek's 1863-64 New York season. *The New Grove Dictionary of Music and Musicians* (2001), s.v. "Jaime Nuno," by Robert Stevenson.

[86] Maretzek had become a U.S. citizen 29 February 1854. His father (or possibly his brother, whose name was also Raphael) followed on October 10, and his sister Rosa, 12 February 1856, and brother Albert, 14 September 1857. His wife's application (dated 1853), apparently never submitted, is in the Del Grosso private collection.

[87] Chapter 2, The Academy of Music," *S&F*, 14.

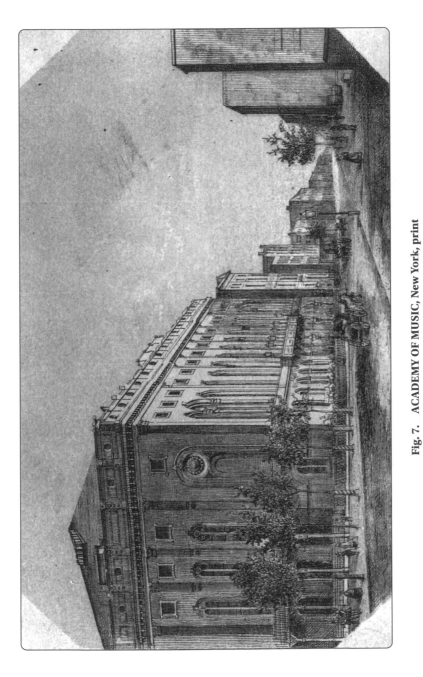

Fig. 7.   ACADEMY OF MUSIC, New York, print

Courtesy of the Branch Libraries, New York Public Library,
and the Astor, Lenox, and Tilden Foundations

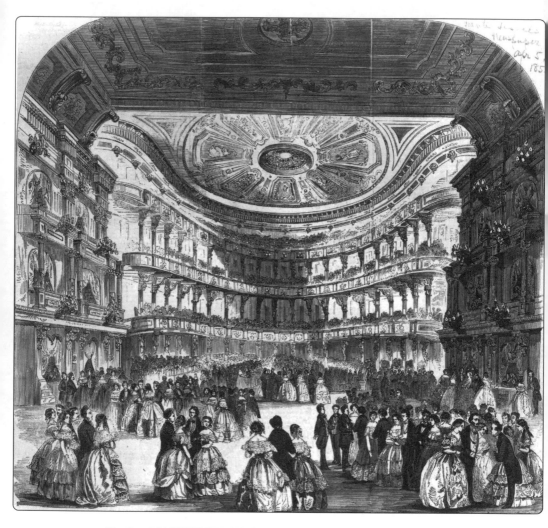

Fig. 8. ACADEMY OF MUSIC, interior, charity ball, wood engraving
(*Frank Leslie's Illustrated Newspaper*, 5 April 1856)

Courtesy of the Music Division, New York Public Library for the Performing Arts,
and the Astor, Lenox, and Tilden Foundations

further, a project using refuse to create landfill between the mainland and the rock outcropping on which Castle Garden was located dragged on, creating a stench.[88] (Plans had once called for the demolition of Castle Garden, but its shell still stands today and is used to house ticket booths for ferries to the Statue of Liberty and Ellis Island. It was used as an immigrant station from 1855 until 1896, when it was converted to the New York Aquarium.) The landfill project was completed as the season was ending on August 25, just in time for the engagement of Giulia Grisi and Giovanni Mario at the same theater.

James Henry Hackett had triumphantly succeeded, after two years of negotiations, in bringing this preeminent duo to the U.S. Maretzek hurried back from Europe after hearing the rumor of their possible engagement. His concern was well founded, for the directors of the Academy awarded the contract promised him to Hackett instead. And so it was that Maretzek took his undistinguished company on tour to Philadelphia, where it soon disbanded, while Grisi and Mario opened at the new Academy of Music on October 2 under Hackett's management.[89] Parquet seats were priced at $3 and boxes, from $12 to $40, prices the opera-going public found exorbitant. Only 1,500 persons attended opening night, and prices were slashed in half the following day. The season closed on December 29 with a loss of $8,000.[90]

1855

Throughout its thirty-year existence, the Academy struggled to maintain solvency. A prime cause of its instability was that, in addition to a season's rent of $20,000-$30,000 charged lessees, each of the two hundred stockholders was entitled to a free seat (one seat per share) or box (four or more shares) for every performance, regardless of whether the theater was sublet for other purposes. The seats were transferable and, once their owners had seen a production, could be sold or given away to spectators who otherwise would have purchased seats. This skimming off of the best seats and boxes in the house made turning a profit very difficult for all who leased it. Maretzek observed that this system prevailed for as long as it did only because of the rivalry among impresarios.[91]

---

[88] Lawrence, 2:508, 512-13, 526.

[89] Maretzek's company presented the last operas to be given in the Chestnut St. Theatre; it was demolished the next year. Gerson, 78.

[90] T. Allston Brown, *A History of the New York Stage from the First Performance in 1732-1901*, 3 vols. (New York: Dodd, Mead, 1903), 2:25.

[91] *S&F*, 12-13.

Hackett did not renew his lease, and James Phalen, one of the Academy's directors, awarded the next lease to Ole Bull, the Norwegian violinist and composer who had come to the U.S. in 1843. He had most recently been touring the country for two years with Maurice Strakosch, Amalia Patti-Strakosch, and young Adelina Patti. Maretzek and wife had joined them in October 1854 after he failed to secure the lease on the new Academy. A Gordian knot of shifting managerial alliances preceded the opening of the spring season. Before the Academy opened, Maretzek had formed an alliance with Maurice Strakosch and John C. Jacobsohn, an importer. They had sent Ullman to Europe to assemble a company. Maretzek and Strakosch soon after formed a partnership with Bull, sending Strakosch off to Europe to engage singers. Bull then accepted a contract making himself manager and Maretzek conductor, but omitting Strakosch. Ullman and Jacobsohn then joined forces with William Niblo, and Jacobsohn and Niblo both left for Europe to recruit new talent.[92]

The Academy reopened on 19 February 1855 with the much-anticipated U.S. premiere of Verdi's *Rigoletto*, featuring Apollonia Bertucca-Maretzek as Gilda and Ettore Barili, Adelina Patti's stepbrother and early teacher, in the title role.[93] Concerns about the plot overshadowed the music, and the farewell season of Grisi and Mario at the Metropolitan Theatre vied with the Academy for an audience. Felicja Vestfali, a Polish contralto hired by the stockholders, made her debut in Donizetti's *La favorita* on February 28. The part was ill suited to her voice, and difficulties arose between her and Maretzek. Bull, in the meantime, proved deficient as manager, and the directors relieved him of his responsibilities on March 3. The directors took a vote of confidence in favor of Maretzek, but Bull did not retire gracefully from the scene. He ordered the Academy closed. Phalen reopened it on March 12 with a benefit for the now former employees. Tenor Pasquale Brignoli, the first of Strakosch's singers to arrive from Europe, made his debut in *Lucia di Lammermoor*. Phalen himself then assumed management, reopening on March 16 with Donizetti's *Lucrezia Borgia*. Balbina Steffanone, en route from Havana to Paris, augmented the company (in the role of Lucrezia). Amid lawsuits and accusations, the first series of twelve performances drew to a close.[94]

---

[92] Lawrence, 2:580-81; *S&F*, 16-19.

[93] More than thirty years later, Max Strakosch recalled that Maurice's recruitment efforts in Europe had taken longer than expected. Maretzek had grown impatient and, emboldened by the recent arrival of Ballcon and Ettore Barili from Italy, had decided to proceed with the premiere of *Rigoletto*. See "Fragments, written by Max" [unpublished memoirs of Max Strakosch], The New York Philharmonic Archives.

[94] Lawrence, 2:584-89, 591, 593.

A second series, also consisting of twelve nights, began on April 9 with a new production of Rossini's *Guillaume Tell*. This was followed on May 2 with the debut of baritone Alessandro Amodio, the second of Strakosch's singers to arrive, as Count di Luna in the U.S. premiere of Verdi's *Il trovatore*. The remaining European talent scouts had, in the meantime, arrived back in New York, one by one. French soprano, Anna de LaGrange (with her opera company) was one of their recruits. In *Sharps and Flats* Maretzek praises her endurance and her extensive repertory in both soprano and contralto roles.[95] A season by the LaGrange company announced for Niblo's under Ullman's management was, after a week of intense negotiation, rescheduled for the Academy, much to the resentment of the Academy's then current occupants. The uproarious season concluded on May 18. The resident company departed for a season in Boston. Manager Phalen and his co-manager, Henry A. Coit resigned, as did their business manager, Chevalier Henry Wikoff. William H. Paine, another Academy stockholder, stepped into the breach. The LaGrange company then went off to Boston in early June, the resident company having returned to offer a weeklong series of benefit performances to close their season.[96]

Paine's first season at the Academy opened on October 1 with *Il trovatore*, Maretzek conducting. Ullman agreed to transfer LaGrange's contract to Paine, resulting, in combination with the previous company and new singers recruited from Europe, including French mezzo-soprano Constance Nantier-Didiée, in an excellent company. Maretzek reported that he retired to his home on Staten Island "with an English grammar, an English dictionary, and an English friend" to write *Crotchets and Quavers*.[97] The identity of the talented ghostwriter who helped pen the witty account is unknown, as is the ghostwriter for *Sharps and Flats* and the third book. The *Herald* reported Ullman threatened Maretzek at gunpoint following publication of *Crotchets*.[98]

1856

Paine's company left for Philadelphia, Baltimore, Washington, and Boston on January 4.[99] Maretzek describes a memorable beginning of the tour: the train on which he, LaGrange, Nantier-Didiée, and Paine were traveling to Philadelphia

[95] *S&F*, 20.

[96] Lawrence, 2:602, 605, 608, 611, 614.

[97] *C&Q*, 112.

[98] William C. Franz, "Island Man Brought Opera to U.S.A.," *Staten Island Register*, 16 October 1980, p. 8; Lawrence, 2:638.

[99] Lawrence, 2:631-36, 640.

(usually a six-hour trip) was delayed by a snowstorm. As the delay stretched on and the group grew increasingly hungry and cold, his servant, hired to assist with baggage, at last confessed that he had stolen a complete roasted turkey and two bottles of wine from Maretzek's pantry, which he had intended to supplement with a loaf of his own bread. All was forgiven and the thief commended for his honesty as the ravenous party quickly devoured the welcome provisions.[100]

The company returned to New York in early March, opening their spring season at the Academy on March 13 with Verdi's *Il trovatore*. The debut of contralto Adelaide Phillipps (Azucena in *Il trovatore*), who was born in England but had grown up in Boston, had to be postponed until March 17 because of her illness. The highlight of the season was the premiere of Arditi's opera *La spia*, based on James Fenimore Cooper's novel *The Spy*. The season was brief and unfortunately conflicted with Lent. At season's end, Paine, who had put up two houses for sale to meet expenses, did not seek renewal of his lease. With Strakosch on tour and Ullman in Europe, the directors prevailed on Maretzek to assume the lease. He agreed to a short season, which began with Verdi's *Ernani* on April 16. In addition to Italian opera, the troupe offered German opera on Saturday nights, with Anna de LaGrange singing the starring roles. Felicja Vestfali, newly-appointed director of the Mexico City opera, had returned briefly to New York and made several guest appearances, apparently having resolved past difficulties with Maretzek. The season, including benefits, closed on June 13.[101]

Maretzek negotiated for nearly the entire summer with the Academy's stockholders over a fall lease. He insisted on two conditions: first, that the stockholders not transfer their free admission to others for opera performances and, secondly, that they relinquish free admission altogether on nights when opera was not performed. He finally yielded on the first point, and the stockholders consented verbally to the second, but were evasive in committing to a written agreement. Pending a formal lease, Maretzek opened the season with *Il trovatore* on September 1 and presented the highlight of the season, Meyerbeer's *La stella del Nord*, on September 24. Having failed in his efforts to press the stockholders for a resolution to the lease standoff, Maretzek took center stage and bitterly denounced his antagonists at the fifth and final performance of *La stella* on September 30. This was the first volley in what was to become a very public struggle, known as "The Merry Thirty Days War," between Maretzek and the stockholders. Maretzek meanwhile made plans to take his troupe to Boston and Havana.

---

[100] *S&F*, 18-20.

[101] Lawrence, 2:680-82, 685, 690-91.

When he learned, however, that the shareholders had resolved, "That no lessee of the Academy of Music should ever be allowed to engage Max Maretzek in any capacity whatsoever, nor should I be permitted to enter the house, unless as a paying auditor," he determined to have the last word. He persuaded Anna de LaGrange's husband, Baron de Stankovitch, to take on the lease and feign reluctant agreement to the anti-Maretzek clause.[102] With Maretzek's "former" company, the new manager opened with *Il trovatore* on November 10 following their return from Boston. Popular demand at this performance proved so overwhelming, however, that Maretzek, who just happened to be nearby and attired in full evening dress, was pressed into service. The baron appealed to the more sympathetic Mr. Paine for repeal of the edict. The directors at first held out for an apology from Maretzek, but finally relented when he held firm. The company offered the U.S. premiere of Verdi's *La traviata* on December 3. The opera was controversial because of its plot featuring a fallen woman. The final performance of *La traviata* and of the season took place on December 11. Maretzek and his company sailed for Havana the next day.[103]

1857

Following the Napoleonic wars, Cuba had become the wealthiest colony in the world. By 1825, the U.S. had surpassed even Spain as its chief trading partner. Coffee, tobacco, and rum were important exports, but sugar remained far and away the most important crop throughout the nineteenth century. By 1845 a network of private railways connected the principal sugar mills to Havana. The first railways in Latin America and the Caribbean were in Cuba. Steamboats were also used for transport by the 1820s. More than half the population was of Spanish origin when the first war of independence began in 1868, slightly less than half were black or mulatto, and a small proportion were of French, Anglo-Saxon, or Chinese extraction.[104]

Havana, with a population of nearly 200,000 and Santiago de Cuba, the second largest city, were thriving cosmopolitan cities. The Teatro de la Reina opened in Santiago in 1851 with a season featuring *Ernani*, *Lucia di Lammermoor*, and *Norma*.[105]

---

[102] *S&F*, 22-23.

[103] Lawrence, 2:694, 697, 712.

[104] Leslie Bethell, *Cuba, A Short History* (Cambridge: Cambridge University Press, 1993), 14-15, 20.

[105] *The New Grove Dictionary of Music and Musicians* (2001), s.v. "Santiago de Cuba," by Robert Stevenson and Robin Moore.

Havana's Teatro Coliseo had opened in 1776 (and was later renamed the Principal in 1803) with *Didone abbandonata* (libretto by Metastasio, composer unknown). A local company presented eighty opera productions annually between 1811 and 1832. The American premiere of Mozart's *Don Giovanni* took place at the Teatro Principal in 1818,[106] and Italian opera dominated Cuban musical life from 1834 to the mid 1870s.[107]

A new theater, the Tacon, was inaugurated soon after, in 1838 (February 28); opera was first presented there the next year. The theater was built by impresario Francisco (Pancho) Martí y Torrens, erstwhile pirate, ex-soldier, fisherman, one of Cuba's first millionaires, and later proprietor of the theater and manager of the Havana Opera Company. Located on what was then Alemeda de Isabel II, between San José and San Rafael, its seating capacity was 2,287, with standing room for an additional 750 (figs. 9 & 10).[108] The name was in honor of Captain-General Miguel Tacón, with whom Martí had collaborated to bring an end to piracy on the country's southern coast and who provided slaves and contributed funds for the construction of the theater. It was pronounced the equal, if not superior to the best theaters in Paris and London, yet critics found flaws, nonetheless. Joseph Tagliafico, a French bass, who sang at Covent Garden from 1847 until 1876 and was a reviewer for *Le ménestrel*, criticized the theater's draftiness, poor acoustics, zinc roof (that competed with the orchestra's cymbals in rainstorms), its proximity to the railroad station housing cacophonous American engines, and the pervasive smoking backstage by the staff. The same article, in the form of a letter to a French friend in Cuba (published in 1858), declares the resident chorus and orchestra "worthless" and advocates the need for a local conservatory of music.[109] The Tacon had reopened 18 November 1846, following renovation, with Verdi's *Ernani*. It was sold in 1909 and the Teatro Nacional de la Habana constructed around the pre-existing theater in 1914.[110]

Despite any shortcomings of the Tacon, Cuba offered a fertile climate to attract touring opera companies. The railroads and steamboats facilitated transportation

---

[106] Ibid., "Havana," by Robert Stevenson and Victoria Eli Rodriguez.

[107] Alejo Carpentier, "Music in Cuba, 1523-1900," *Musical Quarterly* 33 (1947): 371.

[108] Cristóbal Díaz Ayala, *Música cubano del areyto a la nueva trova* (Miami: Ediciones Universal, 1981), 53; *New York Times*, 5 February 1899, p. 15.

[109] Joseph Tagliafico, "Letter to a French Friend in Cuba," *Musical World* (London) 36, no. 50 (11 December 1858): 797.

[110] Jesús Guanche, "Teatros: Cuba," *Diccionario de la música española e hispanoamericana* (Madrid: Sociedad General de la Autores y Editores, 1999-2002), 10:218; Helio Orovio, *Cuban Music from A-Z* (Durham: Duke University Press, 2004), 208.

Fig. 9. TEATRO TACÓN, Havana, in 1853, lithograph, from *Album pintoresco de la isla de Cuba* (Havana: B. May, 1853), plate 9

Courtesy of the General Research Division, New York Public Library, and the Astor, Lenox, and Tilden Foundations

Fig. 10.   TEATRO TACÓN, Havana, interior, wood engraving,
from Samuel Hazard, *Cuba with Pen and Pencil* (Hartford: Hartford Pub. Co., 1871), facing p. 186

Courtesy of the General Research Division, New York Public Library,
and the Astor, Lenox, and Tilden Foundations

throughout the country, and a theater system was in place to present opera to appreciative audiences. *Dwight's* reports the presence of two other thriving Italian opera companies when Maretzek's company returned to Cuba in late 1857.[111] Maretzek's brother Albert died of yellow fever in Santiago de Cuba in 1863 while managing a touring opera company from New York.[112]

Maretzek's company consisted principally of Anna de LaGrange, Adelaide Phillipps,[113] Apollonia Bertucca-Maretzek, Elise Siedenburg, Pasquale Brignoli, Luigi Ceresa, Alessandro Amodio, Francesco Taffanelli, and Domenico Coletti. They arrived in Havana after a five-day voyage. The haste of the decision to go to Havana had precluded advance advertising, but an incident at the harbor involving the rotund Amodio forestalled its need. No sooner had Amodio lowered his considerable bulk into one of the fragile horse-drawn volantes (open carriages, with large wheels) than the tiny floorboards collapsed. The horse, frightened by the commotion, began to trot, and the hapless tenor was obliged to run several blocks along the pavement with his feet protruding through the floor of the coach. News of this scene flashed throughout the city, and the Tacon Theatre was filled to capacity on opening night with spectators eager to catch a glimpse of "E niño gordo" (the fat baby). His audience was enthralled by his performance, and he soon became "the spoiled fat baby of the Havanese."

Following a poorly-received debut by Ceresa the second night, Maretzek was summoned before General José Gutierrez de la Concha, Governor of Cuba, the next morning. The General explained that, since the Cubans were eager for opera after a three-year hiatus during which the doors of the Tacon remained closed under the irascible Martí and since they could ill afford to offer a sub-vention, he himself would advise Maretzek on management of the Havanese public if Maretzek would simply manage his singers. This arrangement proved effective for the duration of the company's engagement.[114]

The company returned to the U.S. in mid-February 1857 for a brief engage-ment (February 16-17) in Charleston and to open the new Academy of Music in Philadelphia, where they performed Verdi's *Il trovatore* on February 25. Maretzek

---

[111] *Dwight's Journal of Music*, 12 (13 February 1858): 367.

[112] *New York Times*, 25 January 1863, p. 5; 26 January 1863, p. 5.

[113] This tour had unfortunate consequences for Ms. Phillipps, who contracted yellow fever and never fully recovered from some of its effects. Anna Cabot Lowell Quincy Waterston, *Adelaide Phillipps* (Boston: A. Williams, 1883), 48.

[114] Chapter 4, "Opera in Havana," in *S&F*, 26-30. Gen. Concha (1809-95) was thrice governor of Cuba: 1850-52, 1854-59, and 1874-75.

subsequently managed most troupes that appeared there through 1860.[115] Italian soprano Marietta Gazzaniga replaced Anna de LaGrange, who had left the company. Meanwhile, back in New York, with Maretzek in Havana and out of the running for the New York Academy, Ullman and Strakosch had put aside past animosities to form a partnership for its lease. It was therefore to Niblo's that Maretzek returned in New York. He opened there with *La traviata* on April 13 for a series of ten performances through May 8, before leaving on tour for Philadelphia and Boston. The timing of these moves was designed to keep the Ullman-Strakosch company "hemmed in and bottled up in New York" and to restrict their ability to make lucrative tours at season's end.[116]

A benefit was held for Maretzek on June 5 at the Academy, before his departure for Boston and then Cuba. It was ostensibly his farewell to New York for perhaps some years. He actually went to Europe, however, to engage singers for Philadelphia, Boston, and Havana in an all-out war against Ullman and Strakosch. He waged a fierce publicity battle against Ullman, who had succeeded in engaging Italian soprano Erminia Frezzolini. Speculation followed that the two companies, which had much to offer each other, might unite, but nothing came of it. A financial panic that began in New York and had international repercussions sent unemployment figures soaring and triggered a depression that lingered into the spring of 1859.[117] After a brief season in Philadelphia in October (5-24), Maretzek left with his company for Havana on 2 November 1857. Strakosch relinquished his responsibilities with the Ullman company (he was replaced by W.H. Paine) to go on tour, and Frezzolini defected to Maretzek's forces in Havana.[118] A rivalry quickly sprang up between the new diva and the previously sole reigning diva, Marietta Gazzaniga. The city divided into partisan camps in support of the two singers. Maretzek did his best to maintain the equilibrium, but a wreath of garlic thrown with other tributes to Gazzaniga following a performance (and probably arranged by her husband to discredit rival fans) struck the fatal blow; Frezzolini declined to renew her contract.[119]

---

[115] Preston, *Opera*, 145; William Stanley Hoole, *The Ante-Bellum Charleston Theatre* (University: University of Alabama Press, 1946), 143.

[116] *S&F*, 37, 41.

[117] Burrows and Wallace, 843-51.

[118] Lawrence, 3:34, 43-44, 57-59.

[119] *S&F*, 32-34. Gazzaniga's husband, the Marquis of Malaspina, died shortly afterward of small pox while still in Havana. *New York Times*, 4 January 1884, p. 1.

1858

Maretzek's company left Havana on the steamer *Isabel* on February 25 for a short engagement in Charleston, before a season at the Philadelphia Academy of Music (March 16-May 17).[120] Despite the addition of star baritone Giorgio Ronconi, who had joined the company in Havana, the season ended prematurely, marred by quarrels, promises of repertoire that failed to materialize, and the resignation of financial backer and business manager, E.A. Marshall.[121] Meanwhile in New York, in another shift of alliances, Ullman, eager to leave for Europe to further his pursuit of London impresario Benjamin Lumley and Her Majesty's Theatre Company in order to compete with P.T. Barnum, sublet the Academy to arch rival Maretzek. Maretzek's company, calling itself the "Commonwealth" or "Associated Artists" was well received, but finished the season (begun May 31) on June 30 with losses and disbanded afterward.[122]

Maretzek had made an advance agreement with Ullman and Strakosch to relinquish his 1859 spring and summer seasons in Philadelphia and Boston in exchange for a fall 1858 season at the Academy in preparation for his Havana season.[123] This season began quietly on August 30, featuring two new singers, Spanish soprano Pepita Gasssier and tenor Luigi Stefani. The season was no sooner launched, however, than Strakosch introduced a competing season at Burton's Theatre with two new stars and longtime members of Maretzek's old company: Brignoli, Amodio, and later Gazzaniga too—a formidable troupe. The Strakosch company initially offered performances on non-opera nights at the Academy, but the competition quickly escalated into a no-holds-barred pricing and scheduling war. Maretzek presented two new productions, Verdi's *La traviata* and Donizetti's *Linda di Chamounix*, in the final week of his season after Strakosch had left for Boston.

Just as Maretzek was preparing to leave for Havana with his company in mid-October, he received word from the Cuban Governor General that the Tacon Theatre was unsafe for occupation, having been badly damaged in a fire resulting from an explosion in a government magazine. Maretzek immediately

---

[120] *Dwight's Journal of Music* 12 (13 March 1858): 395; Gerson, 117.

[121] *Dwight's Journal of Music* 13 (8 May 1858): 46.

[122] Lawrence, 3:131, 135-38.

[123] Chapter 5, "The New York Academy of Music under the Regime of Bernard Ullman and Maurice Strakosch," in *S&F*, 44.

left for Havana and was able to negotiate the use of an alternate theater, the Villanueva.[124] Because of its smaller size, he was allowed to double the admission price. His troupe departed for Havana on November 12.[125] Maretzek describes Havana as "the promised land of managers" because of the ready assistance of the police state in supplying doctors to examine ailing singers and pass judgment on their fitness to perform. A persistently-indisposed Brignoli, facing a "cure" of 400 leaches, made a remarkable recovery in time to deliver a stirring performance later the same evening.[126] *Dwight's* reports a successful and brilliant season; Adelaide Phillipps was a particular favorite with the Havanese public.[127]

1859

Back in New York the following April, Maretzek ran a series of cryptic ads announcing a forthcoming season at the Metropolitan Theatre, which would have competed head-on with Strakosch's company then ensconced at the Academy of Music. The season at the Metropolitan was averted when Strakosch yielded by presenting Maretzek's prima donna for his forthcoming season in Havana, Italian mezzo-soprano Adelaide Cortesi, at the Academy on June 3 in Pacini's *Saffo*, with Maretzek as conductor. The press lauded Cortesi, but persistent indisposition limited her participation later in the season, which closed on June 17. Maretzek presented a brief season at the Academy in collaboration with Ullman and Strakosch from September 12-October 1, before embarking, via Boston, again for Havana.[128] Cortesi created a sensation in *Saffo* and in *Norma*, and Madame Gassier and Adelaide Phillipps remained favorites in a very successful Havana season (16 November-26 March 1860).[129]

---

[124] The Teatro Villanueva was built in 1847 by Miguel Nin y Pons on Zulueta Street between Colón and Refugio Streets. Originally named Circo Habanero, it was renamed in 1853 for the Count of Villanueva, Claudio Martínez de Pinillos. It closed down in 1869 and was later demolished. See Guanche, 10:218-21.

[125] Lawrence, 3:143, 149, 151-52.

[126] *S&F*, 34-35.

[127] *Dwight's Journal of Music* 14 (22 January 1859): 341.

[128] Lawrence, 3:241-45, 250-51.

[129] *Dwight's Journal of Music* 16 (10 December 1859): 296; Preston, *Opera*, 341.

1860

Maretzek returned to New York the following spring enraged at attempts by Ullman to engage the Tacon Theatre to present Adelina Patti, whose debut had occurred under his own management.[130] Maretzek engaged the Winter Garden Theatre (formerly the Metropolitan) and appropriated disenchanted Ullman artists Giorgio Stigelli, tenor, and conductor Carl Anschütz. He added Austrian soprano Inez Fabbri to his Havana roster, and upstaged Ullman's coming production of Halévy's *La Juive* by presenting it first, followed by the U.S. premiere (although in an inferior performance) of Verdi's *I masnadieri* on June 2.[131] The Ullman/Strakosch company returned prematurely to New York from tour, and both companies announced opening nights for April 9 (Maretzek postponed his until April 11). Inez Fabbri made a praiseworthy debut as Violetta in *La traviata* with Maretzek's company on April 12. Maretzek was able to present a series of operas in German because the native language of both Fabbri (née Agnes Schmidt) and Stigelli (Stiegel) was German, and his conductors, Anschütz and Richard Mulder (Fabbri's husband), were also German. The Academy's season closed shortly after Maretzek played his *La Juive* trump card on April 30. Maretzek's season lingered on through May 19, when it closed victorious but heavily in debt.[132]

Undoubtedly compelled by the economic consequences of the preceding season, the former combatants joined forces for the Academy's fall season. A splinter troupe from Maretzek's Havana troupe that had appeared in New

---

[130] Patti made her debut at age eight on 22 November 1851 in Tripler Hall singing Karl Eckert's "Swiss Echo Song" and Nicholas Bochsa's "Je suis la bayadère," with Maretzek conducting. John Frederick Cone, *First Rival of the Metropolitan Opera* (New York: Columbia University Press, 1983), 24-25. Years later, at a banquet in celebration of the 25th anniversary of her operatic debut (24 November 1859, Academy of Music), Maretzek recalled her refusal to sing at her Tripler Hall debut until he remunerated her with a hat full of bonbons, for which he exacted a kiss in exchange. At the conclusion of the anniversary celebration, Patti sought him out with the words: "Max, if I gave you a kiss for a box of candy then, I'll give you one for nothing now!" Henry Edward Krehbiel, *Chapters of Opera* (New York: Henry Holt, 1908), 74.

[131] *S&F*, 47. *Dwight's Journal of Music* points out that this production was twice cancelled, the second time with no advance notice, before an inadequate performance took place at a Saturday matinee, 17 (9 June 1860): 86.

[132] Lawrence, 3:329-30, 334, 340-41. The 1860 census (June) lists the value of the Maretzeks' real estate at $12,000 and personal estate, $3,000. Both are listed in Apollonia's name, perhaps as protection against lawsuits. Other occupants of the household, in addition to the immediate family, were Francis Bertucat, age sixty-three, occupation: gentleman (probably Apollonia's father), and a chambermaid, houseworker, cook, and farm laborer, all of Irish birth, in their twenties and thirties.

York over the summer and starring former Maretzek prima donna Adelaide Cortesi initially joined the collaboration as well. Dissension between Strakosch and Madame Cortesi's husband, Signor Servadio (manager of her troupe), as well as unannounced substitutions, plagued a struggling season. At its close, the company went on to Philadelphia, where the profits of a lucrative grand gala were appropriated by the New York Academy landlords for outstanding debt. The company collapsed in disarray, whereupon Maretzek, recalling his lucrative tour eight years earlier, departed for Mexico.[133] Martí had, in the meantime, sold the Tacon Theatre, eliciting a promise from Maretzek not to return to Havana for two years and, as will be seen, advancing a loan toward support of his Mexican tour.[134]

1861

The entire Mexican venture nearly came unraveled when Adelina Patti, under Strakosch's management, withdrew her agreement to perform with Maretzek's troupe in Mexico City. Fearing bandits en route, she chose instead to travel eastward to make her Covent Garden debut.[135] More than half the profits received in subscriptions had to be refunded at her withdrawal. Maretzek forged ahead, nonetheless, with an otherwise excellent company: Elena D'Angri, sisters Fanny (contralto) and Agnes (soprano) Natali, Apollonia Bertucca-Maretzek, tenors Luigi Stefani, Achille Errani, Giovanni Sbriglia, Enrico Testa, baritones Alessandro Ottaviani and Francesco Ippolito, basses Hannibal Biacchi and Luigi Rocco, and conductors Pedro Abella and Giuseppe Nicolao, Maretzek's brother Albert as manager, and friend Alfred Joel, advance agent.[136]

The repertory included Flotow's *Martha*, Verdi's *Attila*, and the Mexican premiere (June 8) of Meyerbeer's *Le prophète* (the roller skating scene ever

---

[133] Ibid., 3:350-55, 357.

[134] *S&F*, 50.

[135] Strakosch later recalled that two young girls had frightened the young Patti with their account of being attacked and robbed by bandits while on a recent visit to Mexico when she and Strakosch were staying at the Hotel St. Louis in Havana en route to Mexico. He was unable to convince her to change her mind, nor was Martí able to intercede on Maretzek's behalf. Strakosch, "Strakosch and Patti," p. 27; *S&F*, 51-52. Twenty years later, Maretzek filed suit against her for breach of contract ($32,225 in damages), *New York Times*, 16 November 1881, p. 8; 17 November 1881, p. 2.

[136] Lawrence, 3:418. Elena Angri and Pedro Abella were married to each other.

popular), the Mexican premiere (September 25) of Rossini's *Guillaume Tell*, and *Catalina di Guisa* (June 27) by Mexican composer, Cenobio Paniagua. The premiere of Paniagua's opera had taken place two years earlier on 29 September 1859 (fourteen years after its composition) in the Teatro Nacional in honor of the birthday of the president of the republic.[137] The Maretzek production was enthusiastically received, although Maretzek declined to produce an opera by another Mexican composer, Melesio Morales (*Giulietta e Romeo*).[138] The dates of the season were April 13-September 27; Biacchi and the sisters Natali were highly praised. Maretzek divided his company and sent part of his forces, including Fanny and Agnes Natali and Fanny's husband, Enrico Testa, on an extended tour of Mexico under his brother Albert's management.[139] With the remainder of his company, he left Mexico City, where Benito Juarez was presiding over an unstable government, amid rumors of imminent occupation by England, France, and Spain.

On October 31, representatives of the three countries signed the Convention of London for joint occupation to collect debts and claims owed by Mexico. With the U.S. preoccupied by its own Civil War, Spanish troops moved in quickly, assembling off Veracruz on December 8 and occupying the city within nine days. British and French forces arrived between 6 and 8 January 1862. So began three months of tense negotiations that ended with the withdrawal of the British and the Spanish.[140] The French ultimately dominated only a portion of the country, but the major Mexican cities were firmly under their control.[141]

En route to Veracruz, Maretzek's company was accosted by a band sanctioned by General Ordonnez at a breakfast stop in the village of Rio Frio. Their jewelry and small amounts in cash were taken and their luggage was pilfered by locals in collusion with the bandits. Maretzek craftily concealed a bag of Mexican

---

[137] Manuel G. Revilla, "Cenobia Paniagua," *Revista musical mexicana* 2 (1942): 181-82.

[138] R. Stevenson, 197-98.

[139] Guillermo Orta Velázquez, *Breve historia de la música en México* (Mexico: Libreria de M. Porrua, 1971), 330; *Dwight's Journal of Music* 19 (8 June 1861): 79. The Natali sisters, of Irish descent, began their careers in Philadelphia under their family surname, the Heron Family. They studied with Natale Perelli. Fanny married Enrico Testa in Havana, 22 April 1860, and thereafter used the surname Natali-Testa. Ibid., 16 (26 November 1859): 278; 17 (12 May 1860): 56; 20 (4 January 1862): 319.

[140] Alfred Jackson Hanna and Kathryn Abbey Hanna, *Napoleon III and Mexico* (Chapel Hill: University of North Carolina Press, 1971), 38-43.

[141] Robert Ryal Miller, *Mexico: A History* (Norman: University of Oklahoma Press, 1985), 240.

gold under a salad bowl. The company made its escape when the bandits were distracted by a skirmish with travelers from another stagecoach. They arrived safely in Puebla and presented a moderately-successful three-week season there. Maretzek was obliged to invest six ounces of his salvaged gold in a sham certificate promising safe passage to Perote. He later redeemed his investment through its resale to travelers headed back over the same route toward Mexico City from Veracruz. The company gave two performances in Jalapa before at last reaching Veracruz.

Attracted by the prospect of a captive audience of receptive foreigners in a city under occupation, Maretzek's company was able to present only two performances before finding themselves trapped in a city with no audience. With the port under blockade by Spanish fleets and the only means of exit an English mail steamer not due for another three weeks, the company was reduced to eating beans three times daily: black for breakfast, white for dinner, and red for supper. Fever broke out, and Maretzek lay delirious for days, finally recovering sufficiently to plead his case before the general in charge, whom he had known in Havana. The company was miraculously offered transport on a naval ship bound for Havana, and, in a stroke of good fortune for its nearly penniless manager, at no cost other than for food consumed. The troupe arrived in Havana after a five-day sail. Maretzek stifled his impulse to rent the now-available Tacon Theatre and booked immediate passage for New York. His dreams of replicating the financial success of his earlier tour dashed, he arrived at his home on Staten Island with his pockets completely empty.[142] A new Academy of Music had meanwhile opened its doors in Brooklyn on Montague Street (it was later replaced by the present building on Lafayette Street after it was destroyed by fire in 1903).[143] The Civil War had broken out during the company's absence and was casting its long shadow over New York.

---

[142] *S&F*, 49-70. At the request of Maurice Strakosch, Maretzek also booked passage for Louis Moreau Gottschalk, who was in Havana at the time, on the same ship (the *Columbia*) on which he and his company were returning to New York from Havana. S. Frederick Starr, *Bamboula! The Life and Times of Louis Moreau Gottschalk* (New York, Oxford University Press, 1995), 309.

[143] Maretzek later complained that his artists did not sing as well in Brooklyn as New York because of the depth of the orchestra pit and "the Dutch mania for scrubbing." Italian opera alternated with horse opera, after which the stage was purged with soapsuds to eliminate any equestrian traces, leaving the boards immaculate, but damp. *Brooklyn Eagle*, 12 October 1864, p. 2.

Further Revelations
1862

Jacob Grau and The Associated Artists. Maretzek had scarcely greeted his own family before Jacob Grau (fig. 11), new manager of the Academy of Music, was jockeying for his services as conductor. Grau, a nonmusician and the first in a family of impresarios, had come to the U.S. at age thirty-one from Brno in 1853. He had worked his way up from selling librettos for Maretzek outside Castle Garden, an accomplishment Maretzek appraises coolly in view of the absences of Strakosch, Ullman and himself from New York.[144] Although offended by Grau's patronizing offer of a three to six-year contract, Maretzek, ever the pragmatist, agreed to a six-week engagement, to pay off the draft for the company's passage from Havana. At the same time, he vowed to Grau to return the next season with the "greatest and most complete opera company" in tow.[145] Maretzek's first season (two weeks) under Grau began January 29.

*   *   *   *

Mr. Jacob Grau (during my absence in Mexico in 1861 and after the departure of Maurice Strakosch with Adelina Patti for Europe), taking advantage of the situation, united the floating remainders of singers and attempted a few spasmodic operatic enterprises on a smaller scale. Mr. Jacob Grau was more of a speculator than a director, more of a jobber in all kinds of theatricals than a legitimate impresario of opera.

---

[144] Jacob Grau had trained as a doctor, but, because of ill health and "political complications" in Moravia, gave up his medical career when he emigrated to the U.S. *New York Times*, 12 December 1877, p. 8. Herman Grau, brother of Jacob, was also active in New York as an impresario from 1868-95, but in German opera. His sons Jules and Matt Grau managed English comic opera, 1882-1903. Jacob's nephew Maurice Grau, also from Brno, assisted his uncle as a young man and went on to a notable career of his own as impresario and manager during the early years of the Metropolitan Opera. He was one of the first managers of grand opera in the U.S. to retire with a significant personal estate. Robert Grau, *Forty Years Observation of Music and the Drama* (New York: Broadway Pub., 1909), 178-79, 275-77. A second nephew of Jacob (and brother of Maurice) Robert Grau was associated with Maurice, later managed tours for operatic stars, and became a writer in his final years. *New York Times*, 10 August 1916, p. 18.

[145] *S&F*, 70.

**Fig. 11.   JACOB GRAU,
photograph by C. D. Fredericks**

Courtesy of Dramatic Museum Archives,
Rare Book and Manuscript Library,
Columbia University, New York

The artistic merit of his lyric representations were not of such importance to his mind as the sale of librettos, the hiring out of opera glasses, the receipts at the bar for refreshments and other perquisites pertaining to the business. The only novelties produced under his management of Italian opera during that time were Verdi's Ballo in maschera *and Meyerbeer's* Pardon de Ploermel *under the name of* Dinorah. *The musical hypocrites whose stock in trade consisted in abuse of Verdi sneered at the opera of* Un ballo in maschera *and ridiculed the idea of Verdi's attempt to set to music the life of the solid men of Massachusetts Bay in the days of a certain Governor Richard, Earl of Warwick, and laughed at the notion of his sending ambassadors to foreign courts and giving fancy dress balls to the Puritans of Boston. The American newspapers usually ill treated Verdi on account of this opera, and even one of the ablest and most impartial critics (Mr. Hazard)* [probably John Rose Green Hassard] *revived, many years after, this hackneyed subject and joined in the chorus of reproachful indignation.*

The true facts in the case are that Verdi never wrote, nor ever dreamt of writing, the music to any plot or libretto picturing the manners and customs of American colonists. The music to the opera known as Ballo in maschera *was written to a libretto called* Gustave III of Sweden, *a historical person who held a very gay court at Stockholm at the end of the last century, gave masquerades, and at one of them was really shot and killed by his friend, the Count of Ankerstrom. This episode in the history of Sweden and of the dynasty of Wasa was originally dramatized as an opera libretto by Scribe, and, with music composed by Auber, attained an immense success and had a long run in Paris. Mercadante afterwards used the same libretto for his opera* Il Reggente. *Later, Verdi was engaged to write the music to the same plot for Rome, but he counted without the censorship of the Papal government.*

At the last rehearsals, the censor declared that the killing of a European king, even if a historical fact, could not be allowed on the stage, but that no objection would be made to the production of Verdi's new opera if half a dozen or more republican governors of America were to be shot or hanged.

Mr. Jacob Grau bought a copy of that opera in Italy and produced it in America. All he knew about Sweden was Swedish gloves, which he himself used to sell in former days, and all he understood about an opera libretto was to print on the outside "Only correct edition—price 25 cents." If that impresario had had sense enough to restore in America the original libretto, with its historical characters and to put the scene of action in Stockholm instead of Boston, he would have benefited his pockets and would have saved musical hypocrites from showing their ignorance. This instance of changing the text of opera plots is only one of the many freaks of those venerable dignitaries of censorship in the good old times in Europe when they transformed, by their paternal solicitude, the field of literature into a peaceful graveyard.

I remember to have heard The Huguenots *under the name of the* Guelphes and Ghibelines *with omission of all scenes and words alluding to religion. I have seen* William Tell *changed into* Winkelried *and even the* Bohemian Girl [by Michael Balfe] *into a Scotch gypsy; and once, at the time when Emperor Francis I reigned in Austria, one of those learned censors in Vienna erased from Schiller's tragedy* The Robbers *the words: "Franz heisst die Canaille" (This canaille's* [scoundrel's] *name is Francis!).*[146]

The other novelty under Mr. Jacob Grau's direction, Dinorah, *is considered by Berlioz the "chef d'oeuvre" of Meyerbeer, but the public in both hemispheres differed with Berlioz and considered it the least interesting of Meyerbeer's French operas.* Dinorah *has never been popular with the masses and requires a "Patti" or a* [Ilma] *"Di Murska"* [Croatian soprano, who starred as Dinorah at Her Majesty's

---

[146] From Act I, scene ii; Verdi's *I masnadieri* (1847) and Mercadante's *I briganti* (1836) are based on the Schiller tragedy, *Die Räuber*.

Theatre in London] *in the "Shadow Song" to prove attractive. Mr. Ullman sent from Paris to Mr. Jacob Grau the score of that opera, together with a clever young French singer Mlle* [Angiolina] *Cordier* [whose New York debut as Dinorah was the most-praised aspect of the premiere][147] *and a trained goat necessary for the performance of the* Pardon de Ploermel. *Mr. Jacob Grau sent the score to the copyist, Mlle Cordier to a French boarding house, but, enchanted with the goat, he took her to his own home under his special care.*

Not having taken the trouble to read the libretto and having learned that the goat played an essential part in the opera, he could not think otherwise than that the strange name of "Dinorah" applied to the lovely goat. He engaged a special servant and hair dresser for the goat, ordered a fine satin wrapper with the words "Dinorah—this evening at the Academy of Music" embroidered in large letters on both sides of the coat, put a necklace around her neck, and otherwise bedizened, sent her promenading every day through Broadway from 14th Street to Wall Street. This original, although not esthetical way of advertising, saved the opera, which apart from its uninteresting plot and its entire absence of any action during the third act, was indifferently sung. The goat was, for a short time, the success of Meyerbeer's opera. But soon, when the public found out that the goat had very little to act and nothing whatever to sing, the attendance became thinner and the treasurer's cash box empty.

The opera, however, was withdrawn in time, for the prima donna Mlle Cordier exhibited signs of jealousy against her rival, the goat, and accused Mr. Jacob Grau of undue partiality by starring the goat and overlooking her own merits. The manager, however, regretted to part with his new star, who claimed no salary and could be satiated with unsold admission tickets or with empty tin cans.[148]

*   *   *   *

Grau's company, the Associated Artists, presented the U.S. premiere of Verdi's *Un ballo in maschera* on 11 February 1861 and of Meyerbeer's *Dinorah* on 24 November 1862. Verdi had written *Un ballo* for the 1857-58 carnival season in Naples, but moved the performance to Rome when negotiations with the strict Neapolitan censors collapsed. The Roman censors still insisted on a

---

[147] Lawrence, 3:515.

[148] The above passage, beginning "The other novelty under Mr. Jacob Grau," is taken almost verbatim from an interview with Maretzek. Parts of the paragraph, "Mr. Jacob Grau bought" are also included. "Max's Memories," *American Art Journal* 59 (30 April 1892): 93-94.

change in setting and downgrade of the character of the king to a lesser noble. Eugène Scribe had written the libretto for Auber's opera *Gustave III*, or *Le bal masqué*, premiered at the Paris Opéra on 27 February 1833. Playwright Antonio Somma adapted the text for Verdi, although, in protest at the censorship, refused to allow his name to appear on the libretto for the Rome premiere.[149]

*   *   *   *

Havana. *My engagement for six weeks with Mr. Jacob Grau and his hetero-geneous opera company had not yet ended when I received from Don Francisco Marty a letter announcing that he had again obtained full control of the Tacon Theater and requesting me to go at once to Havana. On my arrival in Havana, Marty addressed me, as follows:*

"By your going to Mexico last year and, by my request, refusing the lease of the Tacon Theater, you have indirectly, to a great extent, contributed to the reali-zation of my plan to buy up, cheap, the stocks of that establishment and, according to my promise, you shall now have the management of the concern and I will be your partner. Of the $12,000 I advanced you to carry your company to Mexico, you could only repay me about one-fourth; therefore, you owe me about $9,000. This sum we will throw into the business of next year, and I will take it out of the first profits, if any. The remainder of the profits we will divide. All will depend upon the merit of the company that you will engage in Europe. If the company is good, we will make money and continue our agreement; if the artists, however, should be inefficient, I shall be the loser but we shall dissolve partnership."[150]

After thanking Señor Marty for his kindness, I ventured to say that with money (but plenty of it), a good company could be secured and hinted that he promised to put $20,000 in the concern; and with that sum in hand, I would make myself responsible to engage a first class company and to pay the usual advances of one month's salary and the traveling expenses from Europe to Havana out of the above sum.

"You could not accomplish it with $20,000. I want a perfect company in every detail, no single star, but a constellation of artists. I will give you a number of blank contracts signed by myself, and which you can fill up yourself. This will settle all doubts of any artist about the guaranty or security of their salaries. And, in order not to be embarrassed about the advances and traveling expenses,

---

[149] *The New Grove Dictionary of Opera* (1992), s.v. *"Ballo in maschera,"* by Roger Parker.

[150] Maretzek further elaborates on this agreement with Martí, *S&F*, 50.

etc., I shall give you a <u>blank</u> draft on the bankers Abadoa y Uribaren in Paris, signed by me."

I could not believe my senses nor control my astonishment. That man, who had the reputation in Havana as one of the most suspicious and close-fisted persons in the world, who mistrusted even members of his family, the millionaire who used to count the tickets after a performance himself so as not to be cheated out of a single admission, offering me a blank draft and blank contracts! After recovering my amazement, I inquired whether he would not be afraid that I might succumb to temptation in engaging artists or drawing monies.

"No!" he answered with emphasis, "I have studied you and know that your ambition to get the best at most reasonable cost will prevent you from any thought of taking any advantage of my trust."

Alas! <u>He was right</u>!

*   *   *   *

Maretzek had cut short his engagement for Grau's second spring season to go to Havana in the latter part of March to meet with Martí. He returned briefly to New York before departing almost immediately for Europe to engage singers, as agreed. The negotiations with Martí no doubt explain why Maretzek leased the Academy of Music for six months beginning on September 29 and then abruptly cancelled his season, later departing with his company for Havana.[151]

*   *   *   *

The result of my negotiations in Europe was the engagement of the following artists:

Sopranos: [Giuseppina] *Medori,* [Anne] *Charton-Demeure, Yradier*
Contralto: [Henrietta] *Sulzer*
Tenors: [Francesco] *Mazzoleni,* [Antonio] *Minetti*
Baritone: [Fernando] *Bellini*
Bassos: [Hannibal] *Biacchi,*[152] [Pietro] *Vialetti*
Conductor: [Jaime] *Nuno; and the necessary secondary parts and understudies*

---

[151] Lawrence, 3:487, 502, 511.

[152] Biacchi married Henrietta Sulzer, 21 February 1864; he had toured with Maretzek's troupe to Mexico City in 1861, *New York Times*, 8 March 1864, p. 8; Lawrence, 3:418n.

The amount of money drawn for this truly great opera company from Abadoa y Uribaren in Paris was less than $16,000 and from Negretti and Leoni in New York, about $4,000. These sums included one month's salary in advance to each artist and traveling expenses from Italy to Havana via New York; further, the music for four new operas and some new dresses for Mesdames Medori and Charton-Demeure. The blank contracts, signed by Marty on the 22nd of March, 1862, and by the artists at a later date and filled up by me and the accounts of the bankers, are still in my possession.

Madame Medori at that time enjoyed in Europe the reputation of one of the greatest dramatic prima donnas, and her artistic triumphs from Naples to St. Petersburg and from Moscow to Paris and London were recorded by the press of every capital in Europe. For many seasons, she was the idol of the public at Vienna, and after the retirement of [Sophie] Cruvelli in Paris, Verdi insisted upon the engagement of Medori to sing the principal part in the Sicilian Vespers.[153] *Her rendition of Norma was everywhere attested as the best since Malibran, and her singing and acting in* The Huguenots *created a sensation even in Paris.*

Madame Charton-Demeure, for several years the bright star of the French Opéra Comique and the darling of the Parisians, embraced the career of an Italian opera singer and wherever she appeared in Italy received the enthusiastic homage of the public. Her repertoire consisted of operas of a lighter style requiring a brilliant execution, such as Lucia, Puritani, Sonnambula, The Star of the North, *and others. It is needless to dwell on the merits of the other members of the remarkable company, as many opera goers of the present day can still remember them.*

Don Francisco Marty was delighted when he learned the names of the singers and in each letter overwhelmed me with compliments about my good judgement in selecting and my skill in negotiating with them, predicting a glorious season and mountains of Spanish doubloons for both of us. My dreams of wealth and the castles in the air, which I began to build on board of the steamer during leisure moments on my return trip from Europe, vanished, however, soon. After my arrival in New York, I received a letter from Señor Marty dated 6 September 1862, in which he announced that he had decided upon a "coup d'etat" and to risk with one stroke for us to become either rich merchants or poor jobbers ("O ricco comerciante o pobre mercader")! Consequently he had concluded, first, instead of five subscriptions of twelve performances each (which under my management used to constitute a season of opera in Havana), to force at once a subscription of <u>sixty</u> *performances and to exact the entire subscription money in advance;*

---

[153] Cruvelli retired from the Paris Opéra in 1855 after creating the role of Hélène in *Les vêpres siciliennes.*

second, to raise the price of subscriptions and admissions; and third, to assume the sole management himself, in order to allay any fears of the subscribers about the monies they had to pay at once, in advance for sixty performances!

I had no need to finish his letter to become convinced that *he* would remain the rich merchant and *I,* the poor jobber. Any child can understand that it may be easy to a head of a family to pay $150 to $200 for an opera box every month, but it may be inconvenient to pay at once $1200, and that a clerk may be able to pay for his orchestra stall $25 every five weeks, but perhaps impossible for him to pay at once $125. Besides keeping back and promising some new opera for each separate series of twelve nights as I used to manage, the interest and the curiosity of the public was kept alive. The raising of established prices for necessities or commodities of life without reason or satisfactory explanation has ever been an impolitic move. The biggest mistake, however, in my opinion, was the official assumption of Señor Marty of the management, instead of remaining a silent partner as originally intended.

Marty had never been popular in Havana and his recent transaction of selling the Tacon Theater to a stock company, of afterwards depressing the stock, and buying back the property for half price made for him a host of new enemies, especially among the very patrons of the opera, most of them former stockholders dispossessed by Marty.

And while the public in Havana might have been willing to bestow some favors and show some indulgence towards me [a poor stranger], they were only too anxious to give vent to their ill-feeling towards Marty and did not care whether that millionaire lost by his operatic enterprise or not. My misgivings were only enhanced when, with the next steamer, I received the official prospectus of the Havana opera season with all the objectionable features in it and my name only mentioned among the other persons engaged as musical director and conductor.

The subscription, as I anticipated, fell short of the average of former years, and the dissatisfaction among all classes of society, echoed by the press, created a prejudice even against the expected artists. The public had determined to be severe and the press to be lukewarm (which is worse) with the newcomers. The subscribers were decided to get their money's worth out of the singers, and those who could not afford to subscribe were craving for revenge on Marty by disapproving, if possible, of his artists.

Mesdames Medori [Norma], Charton-Demeure [Il trovatore], Sulzer, Mazzoleni, and Bellini were received with ice-cold frigidity at their respective debuts, but they overcame the ordeal by greatest exertions on their part and finally obliged the public to acknowledge their merit, and after a few weeks, they succeeded in establishing themselves as favorites.

Signor Vialetti, however, did not share their good luck. Having sung many seasons in Madrid and Barcelona and being related to the Spanish composer [Sebastián] *Yradier, whose daughter was in his charge, he brought letters of recommendation from Spain to the Catalans in Havana and to Marty and thus had managed to make a few friends in society. On the occasion of his debut as Duke Alfonso in* Lucrezia Borgia, *Don Francisco Marty and a few Catalans injudiciously gave to Vialetti a reception at his appearance, which was immediately drowned by a storm of hisses from the Cubans.*

Poor Vialetti, at such unexpected demonstration, grew confused, missed his cue, and, overawed by fear, sang his first aria flat! At last the opposition got a chance and were not slow to avail themselves of the opportunity. They soon utterly demoralized Vialetti by their shouts of derision, and at the fall of the curtain, hooted Marty in his box! Next morning, the papers made comparisons between Marini, Bonconi [probably Giorgio Ronconi] *in* Lucrezia Borgia, *and Vialetti in the same part and asked whether the public should quietly submit to paying higher prices to hear Vialetti than the above-named artists.*

Taking their cue from the papers, every merchant on the Exchange, every clerk on the wharves, every lounger in cafes repeated the same question. Still, Vialetti was a distinguished artist who had sung at the Imperial Opera in Paris, in Rome, and Madrid with overwhelming success, and I am sure that he would have redeemed himself in Havana also if another chance had been offered to him. But both Sr. Marty and Vialetti were seized by such panic and groundless fears that Vialetti would rather cancel his contract than appear again in any important part, and Marty would rather pay him and his pupil Yradier the entire amount of the season's salary than to let Vialetti sing again and expose his own person to be hooted in his own opera house.

Without consulting me, Marty paid to Vialetti and Yradier several thousand dollars for canceling engagements, when I am sure I could have settled it by paying only their traveling expenses home and would have received the thanks of Vialetti into the bargain. Marty, also without my knowledge, engaged Madame Ortolani [Mazzoleni's wife or soon-to-be wife],[154] *at the insistence of Mazzoleni and paid her several thousand dollars without the slightest need of another soprano, who only appeared two or three times during the entire season. He also, on the sly, sent for another basso or baritone, a Signor* [probably Vincenzo] *Morino, who came, drew his salary, and never appeared at all, which was a very fortunate*

---

[154] *Dwight's Journal of Music* 22 (14 March 1863): 394. She dropped a Brignole hyphenation from the latter half of her name in fall 1865. Odell, 8:51.

circumstance for Marty, for if the public yelled at him for presenting Vialetti, they certainly would have lynched him if they had heard Signor Morino.

By continued endeavors on my part and the help and ability of my fellow conductor Signor Nuno to bring out new operas, and seconded by the good will of the artists, the season, which threatened to be disastrous, came to a satisfactory conclusion and ended in mutual affection between artists and public. The only really disappointed party was myself who, for a year had worked hard for nothing. Still, relying firmly on the excellence of these artists, I concluded to take the entire company, if possible, to New York where, for four years no complete opera troupe had been heard.

1863

Negotiations with Martí. *Mr. Jacob Grau had already made propositions to Medori and Mazzoleni, but they all gave me the preference, provided I gave them a slight advance on their salary upon their arrival in New York. I was penniless, but, on the hope that still there might be some dividends for me, or with the intention of asking a loan of $5,000, I went to Sgr. Marty at the end of the season, requested a private interview, and stated my desires.*

"It's $5,000 you want? Are you aware that you owe me already $23,000?"

"Indeed! Pray, Mr. Marty, how do you count it up?"

"$9,000 from the Mexico season and $14,000 in the loss from this campaign, which I managed for you."

"For me! Many thanks, Don Francisco, and many compliments for the clever manner in which you managed it. You used me as your cat's paw, by sending me to Mexico in order to enable you to clear $200,000 by your stock jobbing sale and re-acquisition of the Tacon Theater first, and lately by your sending me to Europe to engage artists for you but not for me, and making me lose two years of my time and labor in your behalf and for your own interest. However, I am willing to admit the $9,000 from Mexico, because I really borrowed it from you, but I do not see how you could legally claim from me the losses of this season."

"Were we not partners?" he laughingly inquired.

"If we had been partners and the loss amounted to $14,000, I would only be liable for half of that amount. But from this $14,000 has to be deducted about $6,000 for new operas, costumes, scenery, all of which are in your possession, and would reduce my liability for this season to $4,000. But we were not partners at all. It was you who signed the contracts; it was you who issued the prospectus as sole manager; it was you who managed and controlled the business without

consulting me, and it was you who promised verbally to take the risk of all losses and to divide the profits, if any, provided that I engaged a good company."

"But you brought a bad company!" he exclaimed.

"I differ from your individual opinion and respectfully challenge you to tell me how you could prove legally that I was a partner or that you were only my agent or business manager. Your acts are against you and no proof whatever is in existence."

After a few moments of reflection, he started by asking whether I acknowledged the $9,000.

"I do," I answered, "and am willing to give you credit for it in my counter-claim!"

"That is a good joke," he responded. "Which are _your_ claims?"

"My claims are $1,000 per month for twelve months as your traveling agent, musical director, and conductor. From March 1862 for twelve months makes $12,000. The usual benefit performance to the musical director about $2,000 and for hire of my portion of music and dresses at $500 per month, $2,500, which in all amounts to $16,500. Deducting $9,000 which I owe you, I claim $7,500 balance due to me."

He burst out laughing. "Very ingenious indeed, but how will you now prove your claim?"

"Did you not announce me in your official program among the engaged artists as your conductor?"

"Maybe," he answered more seriously, "but how could you prove these sums exactly as you claim them?"

"Nothing easier in the world, Don Francisco," I quietly resumed. "You remember, dear Sir, that just a year ago you gave me a number of blank contracts signed by you which empowered me to fill them up as best I chose?"

"And you filled one up for yourself!" he ejaculated, jumping up from his chair.

"I don't know whether I did or not, Don Francisco, and if I did, I don't remember whether I filled it up to last for one or two or _six_ years on the same terms."

There was a long pause and we stared at each other, trying to guess our possible thoughts, but at last, with a smile on his face, he said: "I see you are not such a fool after all as I took you for," and, in the most blandishing manner, he added, "You know, I never would bother you about that money lost!"

In the same way, I answered, "And you know, Don Francisco, that I would never bother _you_ with my claims. All I want is a loan of $5,000, which I need to open my season in New York and which I will repay at the rate of $1,000 per night, the first five performances in New York."

"Well! Well!" he said, very amicably. "I shall lend you the $5,000, but I am sorry to see you risk it with such a bad company."

"I will appeal from your opinion to the judgement of the New York public."

He gave me an order for the required sum on Negretti and Leoni in New York, but, for formality, requested me to verify the accounts of the past season, which I did and certified in his ledger as correct.

*   *   *   *

New York, Spring Season. *On my arrival in New York [February 20], I was the first person to leave the steamer [The Eagle], running to Negretti and Leoni and receiving, on presentation of Marty's order, their check for $5,000. Without stopping anywhere, I hurried to the bank and had the check cashed. I was not a moment too hasty, for an hour after, Mr. Negretti received with the mail of the same steamer a letter* <u>countermanding</u> *the order, requesting him not to honor the draft and warning him not to advance me money, as my company was bad and would prove a failure. There was no telegraph to Havana then, and Negretti could not answer until the following Saturday by return of steamer.*

I opened with Medori, Mazzoleni, Sulzer, and Bellini on Friday evening, before the sailing of the steamer, and Negretti, in my presence, answered Marty's letter as follows: "Your counter-order about Maretzek's draft came too late. His company appeared yesterday for the first time. A dazzling triumph! The public enthusiastic and, this morning, crowds at the Academy buying seats and boxes for weeks ahead. The house for next week sold out already. Maretzek came this morning and, without waiting for five performances, returned the $5,000 that I advanced on your order. Yours respectfully, Negretti and Leoni."

Although I never doubted the success of the opera company I brought from Havana to New York, the artistic and financial result by far exceeded my most sanguine expectations. The old spacious Academy of Music was nightly filled to overflowing by crowds, eager to get rid of their greenbacks, which were a drug in the market at that time. The old operas of Norma, Trovatore, *and others more or less hackneyed, drew as well as the new ones such as* Ione (The Last Days of Pompeii), Judith, Aroldo, *and* Macbeth, *which we presented in rapid succession. But I must admit that perhaps the best of these novelties* Macbeth, *by Verdi, proved the least attractive.*

My experience has taught me that no opera founded on Shakespeare's dramas has ever taken root in popular favor among the masses in England or America, and this curious fact has exercised my mind to meditation, in order to ascertain the probable reason of this circumstance. At last I have come to the conclusion that the Supreme Being, taking pity on England and its inhabitants for being exposed to its depressing foggy climate, deprived of the rays of the sun the greater part of the year, obliged to live upon the products of a parsimonious soil, where neither the luscious, spleen-averting grape vine nor the exhilarating tea, nor the protecting and warming cotton plant could vegetate, and, in His kindness, trying to save Britons from becoming the dullest nation on the globe, recompensed them for their stepmotherly treatment from nature and gave them a Shakespeare. Shakespeare became the vivifying sun of the English nation, the food for their soul and bodies, the remover of spleen and phlegm, the transformer of their natural and national qualities, and, since Shakespeare, the formerly dull, drowsy, Britannia, has become the "Merry England."

*   *   *   *

Maretzek's prophetic pronouncement to Grau in the spring of 1862 regarding his triumphant return to opera in New York had taken a year rather than six months, but his company did indeed take New York by storm.[155] Petrella's *Jone*, which Maretzek had produced in Havana, was the highlight of the March-April New York season (premiere, April 3). The New York critics hailed the stars of the Havana company, soprano Medori, mezzo Sulzer, tenor Mazzoleni (fig. 12), baritone Bellini, and bass Biacchi. Medori, while chided for a tremolo and occasional faulty intonation, was praised for her rich, powerful soprano, and her range, execution, and acting ability. Mazzoleni was admired for his beautiful, flexible, powerful voice, his diction, and fine acting.[156] The Academy was filled to capacity almost nightly, and critics described the season as the most successful in years. Performances at the Brooklyn Academy of Music took place, as usual, on Thursday nights.

A brief, disappointing summer season followed in May. Its main attraction, Verdi's *Aroldo*, which premiered on May 4, failed to attract the full houses anticipated and was not repeated during the years covered by "Further Revelations."[157] The weather was unfavorable, and the public seemed disenchanted with opera. The premiere of Peri's *Giuditta* was postponed until fall. A new opera *Esmeralda*

---

[155] *S&F*, 70.

[156] *Dwight's Journal of Music* 22 (14 March 1863): 393.

[157] *Aroldo* has never been performed at the Metropolitan Opera.

Fig. 12.   FRANCESCO MAZZOLENI,
photograph by Jeremiah Gurney & Son

Courtesy of the Music Division,
New York Public Library for the Performing Arts,
and the Astor, Lenox, and Tilden Foundations

was reportedly in preparation for the company by W.H. Fry. The New York draft riots erupted a few weeks later (July 13-16), claiming 119 lives; they remain the largest civil disorder ever to take place in the U.S.[158]

*   *   *   *

Clara Louise Kellogg. [Missing text] . . . *her fate one of the episodes taken from Goethe in Gounod's opera* Faust *and Mephisto belong to the legend; the one a common tramp without purpose, the other a poor devil who lets his victim escape, and are <u>not</u> modeled after their namesakes by Goethe.*

After hearing Gounod's opera in Paris, I decided to produce it in America and would have done so already in Havana but, although as a vocalist Madame Charton-Demeure would have satisfied the most critical listener, her appearance and her histrionic talent did not seem to me to be adapted to the part of Marguerita. I tried to find a young talented singer to whom that role would adapt itself and

---

[158] Burrows and Wallace, 895.

cling to her individuality. After mature reflection, my choice fell upon Clara Louise Kellogg. Miss Kellogg, when a young girl, had been introduced to me by the late Col. Stebbins as a pupil of Mr. Rivarde.

She had a clear, even, melodious voice of great extension, an intelligent face, an interesting figure, and a correct method of singing. She sang on that occasion a dramatic aria from Poliuto. *After complimenting her on her real good qualities, I at once told her and her mother that, by studying and attempting highly dramatic operas, she would be on the wrong track, and advised her to pursue the career of a light opera singer and predicted that she would become a fine Lucia, Martha, Linda, but that she never would be a satisfactory Lucrezia Borgia and less, a Norma. Following then my advice, she made her trial debuts under Jacob Grau in* Martha *[12 March 1862] and* Linda *[9 March 1862] and, having had then occasion to judge of her ability on the stage, I decided to engage her and to confide to her the part of Margherita in Gounod's* Faust, *which was presented in Italian in New York for the first time on the 25ᵗʰ of November, 1863, and repeated since that day hundreds of times without losing a particle of its attraction.*

Miss Kellogg was a decided success and, without doubt, one of the best Margheritas that appeared on the American stage. She sang the part beautifully, with a fresh voice; she looked like a young, artless girl, a real Margherita, and acted in a kind of natural, passive manner, which rather better suited the part than the studied emotional and declamatory activity of more celebrated prima donnas.

After her success in Faust, *I took care, in the most disinterested manner, of Miss Kellogg's artistic development and brought out several operas which exactly suited her vocal and dramatic powers, such as* Crispino e la comare, Star of the North, *and others. Miss Kellogg advanced rapidly in her career and soon became a great favorite, and, if she had continued in that line of operas and followed only the prompting of her then real ambition to attain a high degree of perfection, she would, in time, have certainly become a great and celebrated vocalist. But the injudicious demonstrations and homage of her so-called friends, under the leadership of Col. Stebbins, the awkward puffs of questionable taste tending more to procure notoriety than admiration and no end of stupid flatteries, naturally confirmed to Miss Kellogg that she had already climbed the pinnacle of fame and need not study anymore, while on the other side, a bevy of female relations, from her mother down to her aunts and cousins in the seventh degree, saw in her success on the stage nothing but a stepping stone to untold wealth and, by nipping in the bud any other affection, whether platonic or otherwise in Miss Kellogg's heart, planted and germinated in her brains that insatiable love of money which undermines and corrupts our present generation. Both factions finally succeeded*

*in the evolution of Miss Kellogg from a promising, great artist to a smart business-
woman. Mr. Henry A. Stebbins was the patron saint of the male branch and her
mother (Mrs. Elizabeth Kellogg) acted as high priestess of the female wing of the
operatic propaganda in behalf of Clara Louise.*

*Mr. Stebbins united also in his person the dignities and offices of member of
Congress (by legal election), member of the Stock Exchange (by ready cash),
Commodore of the N.Y. Yacht Club (by hard pull), Commissioner of Central Park
(by appointment), President of the Academy of Music (by choice), and <u>Colonel</u>
(by permission of the <u>alphabet</u>). He used his influence with all persons connected
with his different trusts to make proselytes in the cause of Kellogg, but suddenly
resigned as member of Congress. Probably he recognized the impossibility of
enacting a law by Congress to protect the American prima donna by a high tariff
on foreign importation.*

*Colonel Stebbins was an extraordinary, curious, excitable man, able under
ordinary circumstances to make a rousing political speech; predict the rise or
fall of stocks on the Exchange; to design a new avenue with labyrinthine in-and-
out-lets for Central Park; to defy on board of the flagship of the yacht squadron
contrary winds without seeking (like Admiral Porter) the seclusion which the
cabin below grants; to write or dictate criticisms on a new opera, and he could
accomplish many other things in a skillful manner and in the most rational way,
as long as the name of Kellogg was not mentioned to him. But as soon as the word
"Kellogg" was accidentally or intentionally pronounced, the dam of his intellectual
reservoir burst, the chains of his logical common sense broke asunder, the channels
of his thoughts ran dry, and nothing but Kelloggs remained on the bemuddled
surface of his brains. In such moments, he would utter the most incongruous argu-
ments and absurd sentiments in regard to the Kelloggs. He would earnestly try
to convince you that Miss Clara Louise was the greatest singer and her mother
the greatest wizard in the world. He would seriously sustain that Miss Kellogg was
the better of Malibran and Jenny Lind and that Mrs. Elizabeth Kellogg knew more
about esoteric Buddhism and occult sciences than Madame Blavatsky or the Witch
of Endor ever dreamed of.* [Helena Petrovna Blavatsky was a Russian mystic
and spiritualist who moved to the U.S. in 1873 (and later, India), co-founding
the Theosophical Society in New York. Acclaimed for her psychic powers, the
London Society of Psychical Research declared her a fraud in 1885.]

*This crankiness of the otherwise very estimable Col. Stebbins resulted hurt-
fully to the ultimate prospects of Miss Kellogg, as above explained, caused himself
to become ridiculous, inflicted losses on the lessees of the Academy by being pressed
to engage Miss Kellogg (whether needed or not) in order to obtain a lease, and*

injured for a long time the interests of the stockholders of the Academy, which was hired out and conducted solely for the benefit of Miss Kellogg by her mother, in whom Col. Stebbins had implicit confidence.

*   *   *   *

Clara Louise Kellogg (fig. 13), South Carolina-born soprano, had performed Lady Harriet in *Martha* and the title role in Donizetti's *Linda di Chamounix* with the Grau company during the six weeks Maretzek conducted in early 1862.[159] She had made her debut in 1861 as Gilda at the Academy of Music. Her appearance with Maretzek's company in the first New York performance of *Faust* marked the first major success of her career. She made the role her own over the next fifteen years and sang it in her London debut at Her Majesty's Theatre in 1867. She starred in the U.S. premiere of the Riccis' *Crispino e la comare*, presented at the Academy of Music 24 October 1865. Meyerbeer's *La stella del Nord* opened on 9 March 1866. She was the first American-born soprano to have a noteworthy career in Europe. She married her manager, Karl Strakosch, nephew of her former manager, Max Strakosch, in 1887.[160]

**Fig. 13.   CLARA LOUISE KELLOGG,
photograph by Jeremiah Gurney & Son**

Courtesy of the Music Division,
New York Public Library for the Performing Arts,
and the Astor, Lenox, and Tilden Foundations

---

[159] Lawrence, 3:472-73.

[160] *The New Grove Dictionary of Music and Musicians* (2001), s.v. "Clara Louise Kellogg," by H. Wiley Hitchcock and Katherine K. Preston.

*   *   *   *

New York, Fall Season. The fall season (October-December) featured the U.S. premiere (November 11) of Peri's *Giuditta*, which sustained only two performances before disappearing from the repertoire. The other season premiere, Gounod's *Faust*, on November 25, failed to draw the acclaim that later became its due as the work selected for the opening of the Metropolitan Opera (1883) and the most popular opera for the remainder of the century. The *New York Times* critic found it a work of "unquestionable merit," of "singular interest," "although unequal in its parts," deserving "to be regarded as the most gratifying addition to operatic music" during the past fifteen years.[161] The general impression of the *Dwight's* critic at first hearing was "somewhat unfavorable, but a better acquaintance with it has ranked it among the most meritorious and popular of operas."[162] The *Herald* critic owned to a "feeling of disappointment" and categorized it as not a great work, and lacking in dramatic intensity and "the strong contrasts that make Verdi so popular," although the performance itself and the staging were a credit to its manager.[163] Clara Louise Kellogg returned to the company after a protracted bronchial illness that had silenced her for most of the spring season. She later recalled that Maretzek had obtained the score for *Faust* in the winter of 1862-63 and postponed its premiere until the next fall because of the preference of war audiences for old favorites. An impending production by Anschütz's German company, however, prompted its hasty scheduling in November.[164] The troupe was enthusiastically received on a tour to Philadelphia in early December.

At the outset of this season, Maretzek had stopped advertising in the *Mercury Sun*, a Sunday newspaper with the largest circulation of any Sunday paper in the country. He subsequently filed suit for $20,000 in damages against its editors when they published two libelous and defamatory articles shortly thereafter, attacking his company for presenting a lewd and licentious opera, attracting persons of low moral character to the Academy, and charging that one of the artistes was the mistress of a male member of the troupe.[165]

---

[161] *New York Times*, 26 November 1863, p. 4.

[162] *Dwight's Journal of Music* 23 (12 December 1863): 149.

[163] *New York Herald*, 26 November 1863, p. 4.

[164] Clara Louise Kellogg, *Memoirs of an American Prima Donna* (New York: Knickerbocker, 1913), 77-78.

[165] New York (NY) Courts: Supreme Court, "Max Maretzek, respondent, against William Cauldwell and Horace P. Whitney, appellants" (New York: Wyn Koop & Hallenbeck, 1867).

Music criticism in American newspapers by the third quarter of the nine-teenth century was still rudimentary.[166] Most reviews went unsigned, and critics lacked the credentials for writing perceptive criticism. The exception among New York newspapers was *The New York Tribune*, the most influential daily newspaper in the country at the time. Composer William Henry Fry was music critic for the *Tribune* from 1852 until nearly the end of the Civil War. His enlightened criticism led the way for what was to become a dynasty of distinguished *Tribune* music critics. He was succeeded by Henry C. Watson, son of John Watson, chorus master at Covent Garden Theatre in London. Watson served ably as critic until 1867, when John Rose Green Hassard assumed the post. Even the reviews of these distinguished critics were published without attribution. Charles B. Seymour was music and drama critic for *The New York Times* from 1851-69. Walt Whitman edited the *Brooklyn Eagle* from March 1846-January 1848 and wrote the first of a number of reviews and later essays on opera during this period. He was a frequent opera goer in the 1840s-50s and attributed significant influence on his work, particularly *Leaves of Grass*, to opera.[167]

The New York Herald, edited by its founder, James Gordon Bennett Sr., had the largest circulation of any daily paper in the U.S. by the 1850s. Bennett was a man of strong opinions on many subjects, including opera. While the reviews in his paper went through periods of objectivity, they are also at times a reflection of the feuds and vituperation of the paper's editor. His wife, the former Henrietta Agnes Crean, a piano teacher before their marriage, also composed, and some-times wrote music and drama reviews for the *Herald*. From 1848 into the early 1850s, she may have been the sole critic.[168] She and their children sought refuge in Europe from the tumult of life in New York with Bennett for much of their marriage, however, and it seems unlikely she exerted significant influence on his musical tastes. Bennett was embroiled in a series of quarrels and disputes over the years with William H. Fry and his brothers. In 1855 he lost a libel suit ($6,000) to Edward P. Fry, manager of the Astor Place Opera House.

Bennett was also friendly with Chevalier Henry Wikoff, author, publisher, and sometime impresario. The two had met on a transatlantic crossing in 1838. Wikoff was a close friend of Edwin Forrest, one of the two actors who precipitated

---

[166] Mark N. Grant, *Maestros of the Pen: A History of Classical Music Criticism in America* (Boston: Northeastern University Press, 1998), 62. Maretzek comments on music criticism in New York in *Crotchets and Quavers* (1855), 86-87, and in an interview, *New York Times*, 10 February 1889, p. 6.

[167] Faner, 6-11.

[168] Lawrence, 1:170, 457, 575; 2:60, 325.

the Astor Place Riot. Wikoff had known Henriette Sontag's father and met her as a young girl. He also published a short memoir (dedicated to the memory of Sontag) recounting the curious marital status of Madame Ginevra Guerrabella, who later sang with Maretzek's company. He and Maretzek had become bitter enemies when both were involved in the management of the Academy. Wikoff also was to become an informal lifelong reporter for the *Herald*.[169] Maretzek's already strained relations with Bennett reached a breaking point in 1865-66, when a yearlong feud between Bennett and principal New York theater managers marred the theater season. Bennett's playboy son, Gordon Jr., succeeded his father as editor after the Civil War, but was unable to maintain the paper's prominence.

In Chicago, George Putnam Upton became music critic for the *Chicago Tribune* in 1863. An amateur musician, he wrote numerous books on music appreciation and was influential in shaping the preferences of Chicago audiences.[170] Boston music critics directed their efforts more toward magazines than newspapers during this period. John Sullivan Dwight founded *Dwight's Journal of Music* in 1852. This distinguished Boston-based weekly was to become the most comprehensive music periodical in the U.S.; it included contributions from foremost critics in other U.S. cities, as well as Europe.[171]

1864

Maretzek's company transferred its extraordinary success to Boston, with twenty-three performances at the Boston Theatre in January. *Faust* was particularly popular and became more so when the company returned to New York. By April, Brooklyn audiences were clamoring for *Faust*, with Kellogg (a Brooklyn favorite), but their demands went unfulfilled until October.[172] Thirty performances were presented at the New York and Brooklyn Academies of Music during the year. Laura Harris, an American, made her debut as Lucia at the age of sixteen during the winter season in New York. Reviewers twice noted substitute singers who performed their roles in German in *Faust*, while the rest of the cast

---

[169] Chapter 3, "The Merry Thirty Days' War," in *S&F*, 23; Allison Delarue, *The Chevalier Henry Wikoff: Impresario, 1840* (Princeton: privately printed at the Princeton University Press, 1968), 25.

[170] Grant, 73-74.

[171] *The New Grove Dictionary of American Music* (1986), s.v. "Criticism: 1850 to World War I," by Edward O.D. Downes.

[172] *Brooklyn Eagle*, 18 April 1864, p. 2; 20 April 1864, p. 2.

sang in Italian. The company appeared in Boston during the latter part of March and returned to New York for a spring season. A short season in May that was to feature Meyerbeer's *Gli Ugonotti* ended in disarray when "a few German chorus singers" insisted on being paid for rehearsals, a demand the *New York Times* described as "preposterous."[173]

*   *   *   *

The Company. *The departure of Medori alone would have been sufficient to cause a gap in a well-organized opera company, but in addition to her loss, Signor Mazzoleni and Signor Biacchi and their wives, Signoras Ortolani and Sulzer, formed a co-partnership, organized a troupe, and went to Mexico, where they expected to gobble up the products of all the gold and silver mines of the land and to receive from the government of the unlucky European, Maximilian.*

*   *   *   *

Medori's husband had died in Belgium in the spring of 1863, and she left the company the following spring, following her engagement to be married to a New York lawyer, Mr. Blankman, that apparently ended unhappily, as will be seen in Maretzek's account. In addition to losing some of his singers to the tour of Mexico, Maretzek also lost his orchestra, whose members refused his terms. He nonetheless presented a very successful autumn season in New York, albeit with a new company.

*   *   *   *

Tenors, as a rule, are mean and never believe they are recompensed enough by however high salaries they obtain, but live under the illusion that they are a blessing to mankind, the idols of all the ladies, and a bonanza to their managers. My lamented friend Brignoli, however, was usually liberal and good hearted, and an exception anyhow in respect to sordid patrimony. We have recently been informed that the tenor Lamagno, who received $2,000 for each performance, used to wash his own linen (finding the charges of washerwomen too high in this country) and stipulated as one of the conditions of his engagement that his poor brother be engaged as a chorus singer and, in return for procuring such a

[173] *New York Times*, 30 April 1864, p. 4.

sinecure, requested his brother to serve him as a valet! Although such proceedings may be called niggardly towards his own brother, it was very charitable and magnanimous towards his manager, if compared with the pretensions of a [Lorenzo] Salvi or a [Enrico] Tamberlik, who insisted upon the engaging and paying of an entire harem for them.

*   *   *   *

Lorenzo Salvi, principal tenor with the acclaimed Havana Opera Company that Martí brought to New York in the summer of 1850, later became a member of Maretzek's company. Maretzek likens his imperious treatment of managers to an orange, "to be plucked, squeezed, and sucked out. . . . When the juice had satisfied him, he [i.e. the manager] was to be thrown away and kicked into the street like the rind of the luscious fruit."[174] Enrico Tamberlik, celebrated tenor, had defaulted on a much-publicized engagement with Maretzek's company in the fall of 1857.[175]

*   *   *   *

Mazzoleni, among other things, would not sign a contract unless it was agreed to furnish him with six wax candles at every performance. It was useless to tell him that his dressing room would be lighted by a chandelier and his looking glass be provided with extra gas burners. He stuck to the Italian custom of olden times, before the invention of gas. He regularly received, but never used his candles and re-sold them after having accumulated a quantity.

Tenors are also usually convinced that they could manage an opera troupe better than any impresario in the world and, laboring under the impression that they are the only and sufficient attraction, blame the managers for making unnecessary expenses by engaging good and costly prima donnas and baritones. Mazzoleni, like some other tenors who turned impresarios, soon found out his mistake, and his season in Mexico ended in quarrels, lawsuits, controversies in pamphlets and newspapers, and a general disappointment to the public and enterprising artists.

Of all the principal artists of my great company, only Miss Kellogg and Signor Bellini remained, but, although I felt keenly the loss of gifted artists, I did not sink

---

[174] From the letter to Joseph Fischhof in Vienna, August 1855, in *C&Q*, 164.

[175] Lawrence, 3:43.

under it. I soon succeeded in securing Madame [Carlotta] *Carozzi-Zucchi* [soprano]
from the Scala in Milan (who proved a worthy successor to Medori), Signora
[Elvira] *Brambilla, Miss* [Adelaide] *Phillipps* [contralto], *the very satisfactory tenor*
[Bernardo] *Massimiliani, the bassos Antonucci and* [Agostino] *Susini, and*
decided to pursue my former and well-tested tactics of presenting many novelties
acceptable to the public and suited to the individual talents of my artists.[176]

*   *   *   *

The press received soprano Carlotta Carozzi-Zucchi particularly warmly.
Tenor Bernardo Massimiliani was also generally well received. The bass
Antonucci did not make his debut with the company until the following year
(25 September 1865: Faust).

*   *   *   *

Repertory. *I selected the new Italian version of* Fra Diavolo [December
21, U.S. premiere of Italian version; esteemed for its light and airy music, it was to
become a favorite with New York audiences], *augmented and revived by Auber*
himself, for Miss Kellogg, to give her a chance to renew her successes of Faust, *and,*
for Madame Carozzi-Zucchi, the serious operas of Don Sebastiano [25 November]
by Donizetti and of Forza del destino [24 February 1865] *by Verdi.*

*   *   *   *

A production of Nicolai's *Templar* under consideration failed to materialize,[177]
as did Gounod's *Mireille*, which was reportedly deferred until its reception in
a production by the German troupe because clear.[178]

---

[176] Maretzek may be mistaken that Ms. Phillipps, who was a member of his troupe during the visit
to Havana in 1857, was singing with his company at this time; her name is not listed in ads for the
season, nor is she mentioned in reviews. In *Sharps and Flats* Maretzek recounts an incident from
the 1857 tour in which her father is compelled to purchase a portion of a lottery ticket and wins a
$6,250 return on his investment. *S&F*, 30-31. Ms. Phillipps toured extensively in the U.S. and briefly
formed her own opera company. Susini had arrived in the U.S. in 1854 (Lawrence, 2:516); his wife,
née Isabella Hinkley, also a singer, died in childbirth, *Dwight's Journal of Music* 21 (12 July 1862): 119.

[177] Ibid., 24 (20 August 1864): 296.

[178] Ibid., 24 (29 October 1864): 336.

*   *   *   *

Auber's Fra Diavolo, *together with Mozart's* Marriage of Figaro *and Rossini's* Barber of Seville, *are three comic operas that have outlived all others so far and proved Darwin's theory that the fittest will survive.*[179] *These three operas, after having successfully traveled around the world and delighted millions of listeners, are now as fresh, sparkling, vigorous, and attractive as when they first appeared. They needed no preliminary puffing and heralding such as newspapers and telegraphs now afford, no previous explanations nor subsequent commentaries or formations of societies for their propagation, and they will be enjoyed when the trashy so-called comic operas of today will be moldering on the shelves of their publishers or be used as waste paper by grocers and cheese-mongers.*

In former times, composers who wrote comic operas here and there used to throw in a valse or polka movement, just as a host would serve a Roman punch between the entrées and the roast at a gay dinner, but now one jingling valse is the pièce de résistance and a commonplace ballad, or topical song thrown into the bargain constitute a comic opera. It needs a particular talent to compose a good comic opera, and even men of great genius like Beethoven and Mendelssohn would have failed in the attempt, while the humor in some comic operas of Meyerbeer, Verdi, and other composers successful in serious operas resembles the playfulness and mirth of an elephant clad in jacket and trousers trying to dance smilingly on a tightrope.

But here in America, many young men and ambitious ladies who hammer on the piano believe that they are capable of writing a comic opera. The rules of harmony, the art of orchestration, the knowledge of constructing part-songs or concerted pieces, the routine of stage business, seem to them superfluous conditions. They will string a few melodies together and engage some leader of an orchestra to do the rest for a consideration. I know of an instance where a well-known professional lady called on me and requested me to arrange two songs of her composition. She could neither play on any instrument nor sing correctly, but she pretended to whistle something without any rhythm, distinct melody, or accent. In fact, her whistling was incomprehensible. I took the words of her songs and played something on the piano that came into my mind.

"Is that what you just now whistled?" I asked.

---

[179] The *Barber of Seville* currently leads the three operas in number of performances at the Metropolitan Opera, with 550 performances (ranked no. 13); The *Marriage of Figaro* is a close second, with 418 performances (ranked no. 19), and *Fra Diavolo* a distant third, with only nine performances (ranked no. 186). See Appendix 4 below.

"Exactly so! How quickly you can catch a tune! It is wonderful."

She published the songs under her name, sang them in her own comic opera, and received splendid notices in the papers as an actress, singer, and composer. I know of several successful American operas which have been composed in that manner, but the music of a comic opera seems now to have become of secondary importance. The topical songs, the gags, the scenery, and the dresses are of a higher consideration than harmony, which is only rigorously exacted in the padded and sawdusted links of the girls in the chorus and ballet. Unless a change for the better takes place soon in the taste for comic opera, we may read in the immediate future advertisements as follows:

> First representation of the new opera La cocotte, *composed by the celebrated tailor Mr. Worth of Paris. . .*

*   *   *   *

Auber's *Fra Diavolo*. *No wonder that such delicious music as Auber's in* Fra Diavolo *and skillful treatment of the subject by Scribe should outlive all comic operas written since 1828. What a charming libretto Scribe succeeded in weaving out of the story and fate of Michele Pezza, the celebrated guerilla chief under the reign of Josef Bonaparte in Naples by the Bourbons after their restoration.*

The new government of Josef Bonaparte decided to surround the so-called robbers, and three regiments were ordered to occupy the passes of the Apennines and to intercept Fra Diavolo, while a fourth under the command of Colonel Hugo (the father of the great Victor Hugo) was dispatched to give chase and battle to the bandits who were about fifteen hundred in number and well acquainted with all the favorable positions in the mountains.

After six days chasing, Colonel Hugo brought the patriots to a halt and in a sanguinary battle defeated Fra Diavolo who, although wounded, reached the village of Marcone, in the hope to gain the coast where the English Commander Hudson Lowe had sent an English bark to take him on board. But his escape and safety were fraught with great danger. Six thousand ducats had been offered by the French for his capture alive, or three thousand for his body if dead, and a legion of detectives were at his heels from Marcone to Castelmara. At last, after many days of travel, harassed and bleeding, he arrived one morning at the small village of Baronisi and entered a drugstore. The druggist asked him where he came from and he said "from Calabria." The suspicions of the druggist were aroused by the stranger's dialect and accent, which were far from being Calabrian. He invited him into his kitchen and, while giving him to eat and drink and while bandaging his wounds, his maidservant arrived with the National Guard, who asked for his papers. On his answer that he had been robbed of money and papers, they arrested him and took him to the prison at Salerno.

Fra Diavolo, however, was still hopeful that he would not be recognized, but his good star had sunk. A soldier of Col. Hugo's regiment who had formerly served with Michele Pezza under Ferdinand IV and who knew him well, stood by chance at the door of the French commander at Salerno when the prisoner was brought in for examination. "Per Bacco! Ave maria purissima!" exclaimed the sentinel. "This is Fra Diavolo," and from that moment he was doomed.

Col. Hugo, in consideration of his own services in defeating Fra Diavolo, asked that the vanquished patriot should be treated as a prisoner of war and as Col. Pezza, but the request was not granted and he was condemned to death as the bandit Fra Diavolo. Hugo visited him in prison and, throwing aside all etiquette, shook hands with him before his execution, while Fra Diavolo assured him that nobody but Col. Hugo could have defeated him.

It is said that at his execution he refused to be pinioned and blindfolded and insisted upon dying like a soldier and a patriot. The name of the bandit Fra Diavolo will be known for a long time yet, thanks to Scribe and Auber, but who knows anything or cares for the brave and valiant Col. Michele Pezza.

*   *   *   *

Donizetti. *The opera of* Don Sebastian *was the last outburst of that fertile genius Gaetano Donizetti, although he sketched the opera* Duc d'Alba *and composed* Caterina Cornaro *and* Rita *afterwards, the* Don Sebastian *closed the catalogue of his successful operas and may be considered his masterpiece as regards workmanship. I know that some of the new-fledged dilletanti of the last decade who swallow the ethics of the Teutonic music drama fresh from the keg and who have only heard one or two of Donizetti's operas, wretchedly rendered by inefficient singers (with the exception of the prima donna) and who have been justly prejudiced by the ridiculous newly-patented "Home Sweet Home" attachment to Italian opera, will smile contemptuously and shrug their shoulders when they read any remark that Donizetti was a musical genius, able to write masterpieces. But an author who wrote* Anna Bolena, Lucrezia Borgia, Lucia *(that elegy of love),* Favorita, Linda, Don Sebastian, *and fifty other operas is not to be laughed at; the composer who possessed the irresistible power of convulsing the emotions of millions, to move the sensations of his hearers to the highest intensity of joy or* *sorrow, to excite their passions or transport them to unutterable ecstasy with his music, and whose compositions were hailed with delight during a quarter of a century in all the opera houses in the world <u>must</u> be a kind of genius.*

Donizetti, like Mozart, Rossini, or Auber not only excelled in tragic operas, but also succeeded perfectly in the special branch of comic operas, as the really charming Elisir d'amore, The Daughter of Regiment, Don Pasquale, *and others fully prove. The fertility and rapidity of his creative power cannot be enough admired, when it is on record that Donizetti from 1818 to 1843 wrote and caused to be performed sixty-six operas, besides a lot of church and chamber music and an infinitude of ballads, songs, etc.*

It is therefore easily understood that he hardly had time to execute the material transmission of his ideas to paper, less to elaborate or embellish them with scientific adornments. He had the gift of improvising operas, which seemed to spring harmonized and fully equipped from his brains, like Minerva from the head of Jupiter. Anna Bolena *was written in twenty-seven days;* Elisir d'amore, *to oblige an impecunious and despairing manager, in two weeks;* Don Pasquale *in ten days;* Lucrezia Borgia *in twenty-five days. Still, amid all his occupations and continued travels from Naples to Milan, Vienna, and Paris, he found leisure for social intercourse, amusements, and even for practical jokes.*

Once, passing with some friends a café in Bergamo (his home) and hearing some melodies of Lucia *scraped on a fiddle and accompanied by a cello, they decided to enter and have some fun with the musicians. The fiddler had a black bandage over one eye, a hollow orb in place of the other, and a wooden leg. The other, however, was a boy, sound on his feet and clear-sighted. Donizetti, making signs to the guests, who all knew him, to keep quiet, took the instrument from the cellist and played the accompaniment with variations of his own. The blind fiddler at first listened astonished, but soon stopped short and inquired who was playing the cello.*

"This is not Pablo who just played."

All the guests assured him that no one except Pablo touched the instrument and imposed upon Pablo to say the same. The fiddler shook his head doubtfully and began to play another tune, recommending to play only the accompaniment and no variations, as he would not consent to be second in execution to his hired boy. Donizetti paid no attention to the recommendation, and the angry fiddler suddenly stopped playing. Donizetti immediately took up the interrupted melody and finished it on the cello.

"This is <u>not</u> Pablo!" screamed the fiddler. "Pablo could never accomplish that," and, forgetting himself, he tore down the black bandage from his right eye and gazed in astonishment with a clear and sound vision at Donizetti, whom he recognized.

The clamorous hilarity of the bystanders brought him to his senses, and he broke out in woeful lamentations that his business was ruined, as nobody would now be charitably inclined towards him for his deception in representing himself as a totally blind man. Donizetti, however, took the fiddler's hat and, after first throwing a twenty-franc piece into it, went around with the poor man to make a collection, with good results. The fiddler thereafter discarded the black bandage from his eye, but pinned a placard on his breast with this inscription:

Professor Matteo Bambolini, the virtuoso to whom the Maestro Donizetti played <u>second</u> fiddle.

Unlike Rossini, whose sarcasm in treating singers and young composers was proverbial, and different from Verdi, who covered his kindness of heart with a certain chilling roughness of demeanor, Donizetti was ever good humored, amiable, and desirous to help and assist, even to the extent of abnegating his dignity. Once in Naples, at one of the performances of the opera Columella *by [Vincenzo] Fioravanti, whom Donizetti befriended, the prompter did not make his appearance, and the singers refused to go on without the prompter who, in opera performances gives the cues and signs to the singers. The time for beginning had passed and the manager and author wrung their hands in despair, when Donizetti came on the stage to learn the reason of the delay. Informed of the difficulty, he at once took off his coat and hat, crawled down into the prompter's box, and acted as a substitute from the beginning to the end of the opera.*

On another occasion, Donizetti was requested by a young maestro (who had mistaken his vocation in becoming a composer) to attend the rehearsal of an opera to be performed at a second-rate theater in Naples. Unfortunately, neither of the two double bass players of the orchestra made their appearance. One was engaged at a church festival and the other in libations at the wine shop, which rendered him utterly unable to hold and keep himself or the double bass straight.

Messengers were sent out for other bass players, but the impatient singers threatened to leave the stage and the members of the orchestra to fall asleep, when Donizetti, seizing the instrument, offered to play the part of the fundamental bass and requested the composer to begin and direct the rehearsal. But very often, dissonant sounds, not in accordance with the harmonies as represented by the other instruments, came from the double bass that Donizetti played. At first, the poor director and author quivered and moved nervously on his chair, without daring to reprehend the great maestro, but soon took courage to turn around and, in the sweetest possible manner, asked whether there were not some mistakes in his part through the carelessness of the copyist.

"Never mind," answered Donizetti, *"go ahead."*

The dissonances, however, continued, and the composer turned around again and meekly observed that perhaps there was not light enough at the music stand and [inquired] *whether some additional lamps should be placed near the double bass.*

"No! my young friend, there is light enough," retorted Donizetti, *"and no mistakes of the copyist, but I don't play the fundamental bass as you wrote it, but as it ought to be written!"*

During the first nine months of the year 1843, Donizetti produced three operas: in January, Don Pasquale *in three acts in Paris at the Italian Opera; in June,* Maria di Rohan *in three acts at the Court Theater in Vienna; and in November,* Don Sebastian *in five acts at Grand Opera in Paris. Each of these operas had a triumphant success, and* Don Sebastian *translated into German had a run of one hundred nights the following year in Vienna, where Donizetti directed the first representations in German. This continued strain on the brain of Donizetti caused that disease to germinate which carried him away in 1848 in his fifty-first year.* [Donizetti died of cerebro-spinal syphilis.] *The last time I saw Donizetti was in October 1845 in Paris a few months before his transfer to the insane asylum in Jury. He was stretched on a sofa and, after delivering to him a letter and message from Mr. Lumley, the impresario of Her Majesty's Theatre, he slowly raised his head and said,*

"Ah! They want Don Sebastian *in London and me to direct it? They can have my opera, but not me."*

And reclining his head on a pillow and closing his eyes, he continued, as if speaking to himself.

"London! London! That is in England, the land of fogs and oratorios."

"But maestro," I ventured to say, *"they always have the best of Italian singers and operas there."*

Without changing his position, he answered, "Yes! Yes! Ostentation, not love of music. Englishmen keep the best singers like the best horses, for ostentation."

"Still, they cultivate music and feel proud of some of their composers. Don't you think so, Maestro?"

After a short pause, he turned towards me and said, "All English composers to date are only small imitators of Handel."

Knowing that he was an intimate friend of Balfe, I asked what he thought of him. Without an answer, he leaned back and shut his eyes again. Understanding that too much conversation might cause suffering to him, I rose and quietly prepared to leave on tiptoe; when I neared the door, he awoke and, turning his head, he said, "Balfe is not an Englishman, he is Irish!"

Although most of Donizetti's good operas had been represented in New York, Don Sebastian, probably owing to the immense outlay for its proper mise-en-scene, had been ignored by all former managers until twenty-one years after its first appearance in Paris. I produced it with a splendor in scenery, dresses, and appointments never before attempted on the operatic stage in America, on November 25, 1864, with Carozzi-Zucchi, Massimiliani, Bellini, Lorini, Susini in the cast, and an auxiliary corps of 300 chorus and supernumeraries in the funeral march of the unlucky king of Portugal.

*   *   *   *

Don Sebastiano played throughout the season and again in the spring of 1866. On the night of the premiere, Confederate supporters set thirteen major New York hotels ablaze, as well as several theaters, including Niblo's. The fires were quickly extinguished, although they caused $400,000 in damage.[180] For the most part, New York critics greeted *Don Sebastiano* warmly, if not enthusiastically. The *Tribune* critic noted that the work had found little favor with European audiences, but commended Maretzek for his bravery in mounting the production.[181] The *Dwight's* critic, reviewing the Boston production, found it heavy, unedifying, and unrefreshing, although not the worst of Donizetti's operas.[182] By the following spring, the *Times* critic was referring to it as a favorite.[183]

1865

The company presented its spring season (February-March) at the New York Academy of Music, with Thursday night performances at the Brooklyn Academy of Music. A tour to Philadelphia, Washington, Baltimore, and Boston followed. The troupe returned to New York in early April to present two benefits for Maretzek. He then turned his artists over to Grau for a tour to Chicago for the opening of the new Crosby's Opera House. It had originally been scheduled for April 17 but had been postponed until April 20 because of Lincoln's assassination. Perhaps encouraged by the war's end, the Maretzeks made a relatively substantial real

---

[180] Burrows and Wallace, 903.

[181] *New York Tribune*, 28 November 1864, p. 5.

[182] *Dwight's Journal of Music* 24 (21 January 1865): 383.

[183] *New York Times*, 22 March 1865, p. 4.

estate investment during this period: Madame paid Andrew and Mary R. Mille $10,000 for a thirty-six acre property on the opposite side of Bloomingdale Road (Staten Island) from their home.[184]

*   *   *   *

Verdi's *La forza del destino*. Don Sebastian *was a splendid success and had a good run in New York, but at that time, fashion had pronounced in favor of Verdi's operas and his more dramatic music and more declamatory style of singing. After the great success of* Trovatore, Rigoletto, *and* Traviata, *the public in Europe and America were seized with a kind of craziness for new operas by Verdi.*

Added to his fame as composer, fate favored him by a circumstance that the Italian patriots throughout the country had adopted the saying of "Viva Verdi!" (meaning herewith "Viva Victor Emmanuel Re d'Italia") as their watch and password and countersign against Austrian, Papal, or Bourbon rulers; the name of Verdi was on every tongue and himself the most popular man in Italy.

Having learned that Verdi was engaged then in writing the new opera of Forza del destino *for St. Petersburg, I endeavored to procure the score at once and to present it to the New York public. I had known Verdi personally since 1847, when in London I rehearsed with the chorus his then new opera* I masnadieri *(founded on Schiller's tragedy* The Robbers*), expressly written for Her Majesty's Theatre and conducted by himself* [22 July 1847]. *That opera notwithstanding, having Jenny Lind,* [Italo] *Gardoni,* [Filippo] *Coletti* [baritone], *and the great Lablache for interpreters, and only a success d'estime and a ludicrous incident at its first performance nearly jeopardized its continuation.*

Sgr. Lablache, a large man, six feet in height, and not less than four feet in circumference, sang and acted the part of the old Carlo Moor, who had been thrown in a dungeon by his inhuman son Francesco Moor and nearly starved to death. When in the third act, liberated by his other son, Carl Moor, he emerged from his prison cell and with his colossal protuberance and in a stentorian voice exclaimed, "O mai io muoro di fame" (Woe! I am dying of hunger), the whole house roared and was convulsed with laughter.

Knowing from correspondents how Verdi appreciated my exertions to worthily produce his operas in America, I paid him a visit during one of my travels in Europe and asked him point-blank for the advance sheets of his new opera La forza del

---

[184] Richmond County Real Estate Records: Deeds, liber 60, p. 237.

destino *in the hope that it would compare favorably with* Trovatore *or even surpass it. Of course he refused at first, excusing himself with the obligations of his contract with the Imperial Theater* [Bolshoi] *in St. Petersburg (which stipulated its first representation) and with his duties towards his publishers, but, at my reiterated solicitations, he yielded so far as to give me as a mark of his friendship the following letter to his publisher Ricordi in Milan:*

> *Caro Ricordi!*
> *L'amico Maretzek ti portera questa lettera. Egli desidera combinarsi con te per l'opera* La forza del destino. *Io ho assicurato che pochi giorni dopo la ima representazione a Pietroburgo tu avrai lo spartito originale. Sta ora con te a decidere quanti giorni albisogeranno perche gli amice in America, in tempo onde farla exequire in Carnevale. A Pietroburgo si dara alla fine di Nov. o dai primi Decembre. Egli vuole anche la cantata, che scrissi per l'esposizione e che si dara fra poco a teatro.*
>
> > *Sempre tuo,*
> > *G. Verdi*

Translation:

> *Dear Ricordi,*
> *Our friend Maretzek will hand you this letter. He desires to arrange with you about the opera* La forza del destino. *I assured him that you will be in possession of the original full score within a few days after its first performance in Petersburg. Now you will decide how many days it will need that our friends in America may be able to represent it during next carnival. In Petersburg it will be played the last days of November or the first days in December this year. He wants also the cantata that I wrote for the exposition and which will also soon be sung at the theater.*[185]
>
> > *Ever yours,*
> > *G. Verdi*

---

[185] Verdi's *L'inno delle nazioni* was commissioned for the International Exhibition in London. It was not performed at the opening of the exposition with works commissioned from composers representing other countries, however, because of problems concerning its medium and its date of submission. It was later performed at Her Majesty's Theatre on 24 May 1862, which would then date this letter in May 1862, while Maretzek was in Europe engaging singers for the fall Havana

I showed the letter to Ricordi, but kept the original, which is still in my possession.[186] *Verdi's recommendations to Ricordi were considered a command, and, six weeks after its first performance at Petersburg, I had the second copy of* La forza del destino *in New York, in advance of all theaters in Europe.*

*   *   *   *

Maretzek's company presented seven performances of *La forza del destino* at the Academy of Music and one in Brooklyn, but did not repeat it within the scope of this book. The *New York Times* made note of the premiere before either London or Paris and asserted the significance of New York to the repute of *La forza*, disparaging the size and importance of St. Petersburg and Madrid.[187] The critical reception was complimentary, although the *Dwight's* critic found the plot heavy and improbable, the work too long, and the music derivative.[188]

*   *   *   *

Verdi also gave me instructions and particulars, information about the mise-en-scene, and inquired most minutely about the state of musical affairs in America. Among other things, he asked me whether I ever met Sgr. Muzio, the conductor, in America, who is a relation to his wife, and, upon my assurance that he was a friend of mine and doing splendidly, Mrs. Verdi [Giuseppina Strepponi] *(who was present) asked whether he was making a decent living in America.*

"Certainly," I replied, "he received usually $600 per month as conductor, besides some income for lessons and benefits and is seldom without engagements. Is that not enough for a single man?"

"$600 per month? And how much is that in our money?" she inquired.

"About 3,100 francs," I answered.

I had hardly pronounced the sum, when they both, Mr. and Mrs. Verdi, jumped up in astonishment and he exclaimed at the top of his voice: "Tell him to remain in America by all means and never to return to Europe." I give the same advice now to a certain conductor <u>*now*</u> *in New York.*

---

season in partnership with Martí. For the premiere, Mme Tietjens replaced Tamberlik in the tenor solo, and Luigi Arditi conducted. Mary Jane Phillips-Matz, *Verdi: A Biography* (New York: Oxford University Press, 1993), 46-48.

[186] The autograph manuscript of this letter does not appear to have survived.

[187] *New York Times*, 24 February 1865, p. 4.

[188] *Dwight's Journal of Music* 24 (4 March 1865): 405; (18 March 1865): 414.

*   *   *   *

Emanuele Muzio, later executor of Verdi's will, failed to heed the composer's advice, returning to Europe the next year (1866), following his marriage to singer Lucy Simmons. He had conducted the U.S. premiere of *Un ballo in maschera*, presented by Grau in 1861, and had conducted at Havana's Tacon Theater in 1862. He later returned to the U.S. for the premiere of *Aida* (1873). Muzio gave the French premiere of *La forza del destino* in 1876, and was again in Havana in 1878-79.[189]

*   *   *   *

Although in possession of the score, the production of Forza del destino *in New York was retarded by the run of* Faust, Ione, *and* Don Sebastian *until the following season of 1864-65, when in February* [24th] *of that year its first representation took place with Madame Carozzi-Zucchi, Miss* [Catarina] *Morensi,*[190] *Sgrs. Massimiliani, Bellini, Lorini, and Susini in the cast and with a brilliant mise-en-scene. Several arias and the camp scene, literally transferred from Schiller's* Wallensteins Lager *(the* Camp of Wallenstein*), won enthusiastic applause, but the expectations of a revival of another* Trovatore *furor were doomed to disappointment.*

*   *   *   *

Ford's Theater, Washington, D.C. *Whether the air in St. Petersburg, where he composed the greater portion of that opera, acted depressingly on Verdi's creative power, just as the gloomy climate of London affected him when he wrote* I masnadieri, *or whether the senseless libretto could not inspire him, the opera of* Forza del destino *never attained any popularity here or elsewhere. Still, this opera finished one of the most successful opera seasons, to the surprise of the public and even of the manager who, owing to the absence of Medori, Mazzoleni, Biacchi,*

---

[189] *The New Grove Dictionary of Music and Musicians* (2001), s.v. "Emanuele Muzio," by Gustavo Marchesi.

[190] Morensi was a pseudonym used by Kate Duckworth; she was married to Pasquale Brignoli. Krehbiel, *Chapters of Opera*, 82-83.

felt nervous at the beginning of that operatic campaign. After its close on the 23rd of March, 1865, Mr. John Ford (manager of the opera houses in Washington and Baltimore) engaged my entire company to give opera performances for one week in each of these cities, and we opened in the first week in April in Ford's Theater in Washington. The capitol was crowded at that time, just after the second presidential inauguration of Abraham Lincoln, and manager Ford did a splendid business.

For the first night of La forza del destino *it was announced that President Lincoln would visit the opera. After rehearsal in the afternoon, a young, fashion-ably-dressed gentleman accosted me in leaving the orchestra and introduced himself as Mr. Wilkes Booth, brother of Edwin Booth. Believing that he desired the courtesies of the profession extended to him, I told him he might come to hear the opera whenever he liked but that I could not procure him a seat for that night, as every available seat in the house was taken in anticipation of Mr. Lincoln's visit.*

"Then it is true that he will come tonight?" he inquired.

"So I am informed by Mr. Ford," I answered.

"Which box will he occupy?"

"I do not know! Mr. Ford is boss of the house, but I suppose one or both of the proscenium boxes are to be reserved for him and his party."

"Will they be decorated for the occasion?" he continued to ask.

"You must ask Mr. Ford! I cannot tell!"

"Oh, something must be done to give him a splendid reception. I will look at these boxes and take measures for decorations."

With these words, he left me and went to examine the boxes. The President did not come that evening, or any other evening during that opera week, but Wilkes Booth was seen every night, either in the lobbies or in the bar room. Ten days after our departure from Washington, President Lincoln went to that theater to witness a dramatic performance and met his tragic death at the hands of the same Wilkes Booth.

Although terror-stricken when I heard the sad news, I thanked my stars that Lincoln did not visit the opera and saved me and the opera from disgraceful notoriety and perhaps even from investigation and accusation if the catastrophe had taken place during a performance of the Italian opera, as Wilkes Booth had evidently meditated. [President Lincoln was assassinated on Good Friday, April 14, following the fall of Richmond and the surrender at Appomattox earlier the same month. He died the next morning. On April 24-25 his funeral train stopped for his body to lie in state in New York, one of several stops en route to Springfield.]

*   *   *   *

Maretzek sailed for Europe in June 1865, returning in late August with six new artists: Enrichetta Bosio, soprano; Bine de Rossi, contralto; Ettore Irfrè, tenor; Giuseppe Marra, baritone; G. B. Antonucci, bass; and Agostino Rovere, buffo, who had come to the U.S. with Alboni in 1853. Rovere died suddenly in December at age sixty, following a three-day illness. Antonucci, who had been a hit in Paris, was a particular coup. The return of Mazzoleni and his wife, Antonietta Ortolani, from their Mexican adventures and the addition of the opera chorus from Anschütz's German company, as well as twelve male voices from Her Majesty's Theatre in London, further strengthened an already formidable company. The fall season in New York opened in late September and ran through mid-December, after which the company went on tour to Baltimore, Washington, Philadelphia, Boston, and Hartford. Meyerbeer's *L'Africana* and the Riccis' *Crispino e la comare* were the two premieres for the season. Plans to present Petrella's *Foletto di gesly* (*Will-o-the-wisp*), written for Bosio, his former pupil, failed to materialize.

*   *   *   *

Meyerbeer's *L'Africaine*. *During the summer of 1865, the operatic sensation in Paris was Meyerbeer's posthumous opera of* L'Africaine. *Although posthumous, it was not incomplete, as Meyerbeer had it finished for many years and, pursuant to his custom, had made many changes, variants, additions, or cuts of his original score and some scenes even composed twice in different manner.*

That bulk of manuscript was confided to Mr. Fétis to select from it what he thought best and to arrange and prepare the opera for its production in Paris. Mr. Fétis was a professional musical critic who had studied and expounded the theories of music, but who could never fully understand that mathematics is only one *of the laws of music, but not music itself. He was often nicknamed Mr. Foetus for the ill-savor of his criticisms, but more respected than many other self-styled musical critics who, unable to explain the difference between a three-four movement from one in six-eight (although 3/4 are equal to 6/8 in mathematics), would declare that a certain phrase in some musical work describes the growing of the grass and that such motif represents the sliding of grains of gold in the bottom of a river, or that a certain tremolo figure on the double basses sustained by clarinets and horns is a depicture of the chemical process of producing petroleum in the bowels of the earth.* [Meyerbeer himself selected the Belgian writer and composer François-Joseph Fétis to prepare the final version of *L'Africaine* for the first performance on 28 April 1865, at the Paris Opéra.]

The essence of music after all is inspiration, revelation, part of the infinite, which needs time but no space, and the only real criticism of music, based upon the psychical or intellectual emotions it produces, is a science of experience. With the immense material on hand, Mr. Fétis could not fail to arrange satisfactorily the opera of L'Africaine, and it proved a great success, but those who ever witnessed how Meyerbeer rehearsed his operas, how he repeated every piece in different ways to obtain the best effect, in fact, how he nearly re-composed his work during rehearsals, must deeply regret his premature death. [Meyerbeer died 2 May 1864, in Paris, after a brief illness.]

The vivifying spark with which he animated his operas at rehearsal was wanting, and L'Africaine, *though a great and successful work, will never compare with* Robert le diable, The Huguenots, *or* The Prophète, *nor did the libretto offer musical situations and other opportunities like those in the above-named operas. The immense talent, the particular individuality of the genius of Meyerbeer consisted chiefly in his ability to express most powerfully contrasts, such as the diabolical element against the angelic in* Robert le diable, *the religious simplicity of Calvinism against Catholic fanaticism in* The Huguenots, *and to draw the characters of his heroines and heroes in a striking and unmistakable manner. How true and beautiful the musical portrayed of a sisterly love in* Robert le diable; *how passionate and soul stirring that of a woman's love and sacrifice for the man of her choice in* The Huguenots, *and how noble, pathetic, and dignified that of a mother's love for her deluded son in* The Prophète!

Meyerbeer may also be called the inventor of the "leading melody," not to be confounded with the leit motif *used so prominently by Richard Wagner, and of which C. M. von Weber was the first inventor. The first* leit motif *ever used occurs in the twenty-sixth or twenty-seventh bar* [the Samiel diminished seventh begins in measure 26] *in the overture of* Freischütz *and is the* leit motif *of "Samuel;" it is repeated at every appearance of the wild hunter. The "leading melody" (not a single phrase) in* The Huguenots *is the Chorale of Martin Luther; in* Robert le diable, *the ballad of the Norman legend about Robert's mother and the Demon; and in* The Prophète, *the coronation chorale sung by the choirboys.*

Meyerbeer's was the musical genius of his time, and each time produces men of talent adapted to the requirements of the epoch, or perhaps each genius is modeling his thought according to the state of affairs or the questions that agitate his era. Of course, men like Homer and Shakespeare are exceptions. They not only anticipate their time, but are for all times; but to date, the greatest and most genial musical composers only reflected in their works the minds and emotions of their contemporaries and the spirit or the doctrines of the epoch they lived in.

Mozart was living under the blessed reign of Josef II of Austria, and on the waves of Mozart's music you are gliding comfortably and take delight in the pleasures of peace and the joys of love and feel sensations of a longing for eternal bliss.[191] Beethoven, contemporarily with the great political revolution of his time, created a revolution of his own in music by his gigantic genius. Beethoven was the Napoleon of music. During the fictitious calm and the careless abandon that pervaded Europe during the Restoration [under Louis XVIII in 1814], *Rossini grasped the scepter of the realm of music, and his compositions reflect the Epicurean sensuality of his epoch. Melody pure and simple reigns supreme to the detriment of harmony and intellectual conceptions. Awakening from the illusionary dreams of a fallacious peace, the nations rose again in 1830, and, during the revolutionary movements of that and the following years, questions of social problems coming to the surface caused the public to become more serious and fully satiated with the* dolce-far-niente *in Rossini's music; they craved for something more substantial than sweetmeats in dramatic music.*

Then Meyerbeer, understanding the situation, discarded Rossinian theories and mounted the throne of the empire of music by uniting melody with harmony and treating musically, with marked brilliancy and success, religious and social issues in The Huguenots *and in* The Prophète. *When Meyerbeer was at the zenith of his glory, two young Germans were treading the boulevards in Paris, the one vainly trying to get a hearing of an overture for orchestra at the concerts of the Conservatory and the other offering an operetta in one act to a subterranean café chantant in the Palais Royale.*

The first of these aspirants to musical fame became afterwards known as Richard Wagner and his overture as that of Rienzi *and the second as Jacques Offenbach and his operetta* Les deux aveugles, *and Meyerbeer, who received them occasionally at his residence, never dreamed that these two young authors were destined to play an important part in the musical world and still less that Wagner and Offenbach would ever be able to* [change?] *directions to make a sweeping revolution in the musical taste of Europe and shake the foundation of the old-fashioned historical music dramas.*

Wagner's genius manifested itself by the indomitable courage and perseverance with which he destroyed the stereotyped conventionalities of the old French and Italian operas, by the boldness of his surprising harmonies, and the colossal combinations of his instrumentation. His music dramas are the overthrow, the nihilism of all former institutions, and his musical delineations a mirror of Schoppenhauer's

---

[191] Joseph II, Emperor of Austria, 1756-90, composed and also played several instruments. Mozart received a court appointment as a chamber musician in 1787.

pessimism in German, while Offenbach, caricaturing the old forms of opera, invented ironical music with the can-can as principal element which photographed the Sybaritism and corruption of the same epoch in France.

The opera of L'Africaine *was performed at the time when both Wagner's theories were already accepted in Germany and Offenbach's operettas were the rage in Paris. Therefore, in Germany many consider Meyerbeer's late opera as a shallow composition while others in France pronounce it as too scientific. Still,* L'Africaine *has passed its four hundredth representation in Paris and proved a success in every capitol in Europe.*

At the time of its first production, Wagner's music had not yet taken hold in New York and Offenbach's operettas were entirely unknown. I concluded to present it at once in New York, and a few months only after its first representation in Paris, it was sung in New York on the first day of December 1865, with a gorgeous mise-en-scene, stage decorations, machinery, dresses after models from the Paris Academy of Music, and with a cast not inferior to that in the French capitol.

Mazzoleni, who had returned from Mexico like the prodigal son, was received with open arms by the manager and the public, and he proved as good a Vasco di Gama as [Emilio] Naudin in Paris. Madame Carozzi-Zucchi, Sgr. Ortolani, Bellini, Antonucci, and others could all favorably compare with the singers in Paris. L'Africaine *took New York by storm and extra performances had to be given to satisfy the demands for admission, and here is the reproduction of a portion of the report from the* New York Times *of 4 December 1865:*

> The African *on Saturday night attracted another splendid house, different in its elements, we need scarcely say, to the ordinary audiences, for Saturday has not yet been taken into the good graces of our fashionable theatre goers. The appreciation of this numerous jury served as another verdict in favor of Meyerbeer's work. By prudently ignoring the demonstrations of the audience, and resisting many urgent demands for "encores," the performance was brought to an end shortly after eleven o'clock.*
>
> *The "entr'actes" were unusually brief in view of the amount of work that had to be done on the stage, and the work, it must be added, is done thoroughly. It is no exaggeration to say that* The African *is the best produced opera ever given in New York.*
>
> *The scenery is so good that Mr. Calyo (the artist) enjoys the pleasure of a nightly recall before the curtain. In other particulars, such as the costumes, appointments, etc., the*

liberality of Mr. Maretzek is so conspicuous that he too is brought forward for a round of hearty applause. The artists are used to this kind of treatment and enjoy an excess of favor, being brought before the curtain after each act. In all respects, indeed the warmth of approval is without parallel.

No opera by Meyerbeer has ever been produced with such immediate acceptance on the part of the public.

The performance on Saturday night was in every way admirable. The singers were all in fine voice, and the ensembles were rendered with the most perfect precision.

Meyerbeer's opera and Ricci's comic opera of Crispino e la comare (The Cobbler and the Fairy) *with Miss Kellogg and the great buffo Rovere, carried the entire season of 1865-66, which may be recorded as the most brilliant since the introduction of opera in America. At last Italian opera seemed to be established on a permanent and firm basis.*

The latest and best operas had been presented regardless of cost, celebrated artists had been engaged, native talent such as Miss Kellogg, Miss Laura [Drake] Harris, Miss Stella Bonheur, Mrs. [Jennie R.] Van Zandt, Morensi, [Adelaide] Phillips, and others had been encouraged—Minnie Hauck, Mrs. [Marie-Louise] Durand (afterwards celebrated artists)[192] *had been trained and prepared under the auspices of the manager for the stage; the charter of the Academy of Music had thus therefore been carried out by me alone, without any other help from the stockholders, except their adherence to free boxes and seats and to their strict observance of receiving their rent without delay.*

---

[192] Van Zandt's daughter Marie was even better known. She was lauded in Paris in the 1880s and created the title role in Delibes's *Lakmé*. She later sang in the U.S. as well. Amalia Mignon Hauck (Minnie Hauk) was indeed celebrated. Maretzek's company performed the first opera she heard (Kellogg in Auber's *Fra Diavolo* at the Academy), and she auditioned for Maretzek shortly after. She made a private debut in Donizetti's *Linda di Chamounix* at Leonard Jerome's theater and her public debut at age fourteen under Maretzek at the Brooklyn Academy (after the fire at the New York Academy), singing Amina in Bellini's *La sonnambula* (13 October 1866). The following month she made her New York debut at the Winter Garden as Prascovia in Meyerbeer's *La stella del Nord*. Hauk recalls in her memoirs that she persuaded Maretzek to substitute her for Angela Peralta (who was slow to learn the part) as Juliette in the U.S. premiere of Gounod's *Romeo e Giulietta* (15 November 1867). Hauk later dropped her first name and the c from Hauck. She studied in Paris with Maurice Strakosch and sang throughout Europe, singing mezzo roles later in her career. Her home in later life was in Triebschen, near Lucerne, in a house once occupied by Wagner. Minnie Hauk, *Memories of a Singer* (New York: Arno, 1977), 29-38. Durand's career is less clearly documented. Her appearances with Maretzek's German and Italian troupes at Chicago's

*　　*　　*　　*

After *Faust, Crispino* and *L'Africaine* were the most popular operas presented by Maretzek's company during the period covered by "Further Revelations." The quality of the company was doubtless a prime factor. Rovere and Kellogg were immensely popular in *Crispino,* which, although now fallen into oblivion, was an immediate hit with audiences, perhaps because its light frothy music offered respite from the war. The *Tribune* hailed *L'Africaine* as the triumph of Maretzek's career, congratulating him at the same time on the most successful opera season ever in New York.[193]

It was during this extraordinary fall season that Maretzek and other managers of leading New York theaters stopped advertising in the *New York Herald.* In his autobiography, P. T. Barnum takes credit for instigating the quarrel with the editor James Gordon Bennett, whereas other observers attribute responsibility to Maretzek. An editorial on September 26 describes Maretzek as "a blackguard and a common liar."[194] The *Herald* reviews, which, in previous seasons, had been generally laudatory and supportive of Maretzek's company, abruptly changed tone. The critic became outrageously pro-Grau and anti-Maretzek, and, after a series of attacks on the new singers and particularly their manager, reviews of Maretzek's company ceased altogether, replaced by coverage of Grau's company in Chicago, St. Louis, Havana, or wherever they might have been.

A brief piece that appeared with more general news in a late 1865 issue reported that "London, Paris, St. Petersburg and Chicago are now the great operatic centers of the world. It is a matter of regret to all who take pride in New York City that Chicago, a city of yesterday, should surpass us in opera and that we should be compelled to take the sweepings of third rate companies from Europe."[195] Maretzek drew laughter from his audience at the season's final evening performance (*L'Africaine,* at which he was presented with a silver tea service) with the observation that he no longer advertised in the *Herald.*[196] A truce was declared on all sides at the end of the spring 1866 season.

Crosby's Opera House in 1868 are noted in Eugene Cropsey, *Crosby's Opera House: Symbol of Chicago's Cultural Awakening* (Madison, NJ: Fairleigh Dickinson University Press, 1999), 226-27.

[193] *New York Tribune,* 8 December 1865, p. 8.

[194] Odell, 8:1.

[195] *New York Herald,* 16 November 1865, p. 4.

[196] *New York Times,* 16 December 1865, p. 4. This may be the same silver tea service (engraved with an M) that Antoinette Maretzek Lindsay bequeathed to the Metropolitan Museum of Art (although the gift was not accepted; cf. Barbara File, Archivist, telephone communication, 29 August 2001).

1866

New York, Spring Season. The New York spring season of 1866 (February-mid April) continued the momentum of the fall season. The *Brooklyn Eagle* declared it, both financially and artistically, the most successful season ever in Brooklyn.[197] Three new singers joined the company: Carmelina Poch, soprano; Felice Brandini, baritone; and buffo Ardovona Sarti, who replaced Rovere. Two revivals, both by Meyerbeer and capitalizing on the success of *L'Africaine*, were presented: *La stella del Nord*, featuring the popular Clara Louise Kellogg, and *Gli Ugonotti*.

*   *   *   *

The famous opera balls were also launched during that season by me, and the first one [April 5], *with about one hundred caricatures of the most prominent men of America by T*[homas] *Nast serving as decorations, was the great social event of the carnival of 1866.*[198] *Only a limited number of tickets were issued and those could only be obtained from the leaders of society, such as* [August] *Belmont* [financier, politician, sportsman, first board president of the Academy, 1878-84], *Stebbins,* [William Wheelwright] *Skiddy* [manufacturer], [Francis Channing] *Barlow* [lawyer and soldier], [James Carson] *Brevoort* [engineer and rare books collector], *Leonard Jerome* [financier, sportsman, and future grandfather of Winston Churchill], *Chas. Morgan* [shipping and railroad magnate], [Francis Brockholst] *Cutting* [lawyer and politician], [William Riggin] *Travers* [former partner of L. Jerome; founder of Lyndhurst, New Jersey], *Henry Clews* [banker, an agent of U.S. government in marketing bonds that financed the Civil War], *etc.*

This evidently shows that Mr. Ward McAllister is neither the inventor nor the discoverer of New York society. The number of admissible families had not yet reached four hundred, but they consisted really of the crème de la crème of society, and, although a gay crowd, behaved in a most distinguished manner at these balls, while Mr. Ward McAllister's admixture (to judge from the excesses at

---

[197] *Brooklyn Eagle*, 16 March 1866, p. 3.

[198] Nast was on the staff of *Harper's Weekly*, 1862-86. His eloquent drawings during the Civil War launched the political role of the American cartoon. He created the image of Santa Claus accompanying the Clement Clark Moore poem, "The Night before Christmas," published in *Harpers*, 1862, and the donkey and elephant symbols for the Democratic and Republican parties.

his last ball at the Metropolitan Opera House) seems to have turned that crème into Limburger cheese.[199]

The so-called society of that epoch, although an exclusive and monied aristo-cratic body, possessed good taste, education, refined, well-bred customs, and treated men of literary or musical talent on an equal footing with themselves, according to European fashion, but many of those who have since received from Mr. Ward McAllister a diploma of admissibility in New York society believe themselves far above poets, composers, great singers, or tragedians.

Exceptions, however, have been allowed in favor of Miss Christine Nilsson or Mr. Paul Kalisch and some few others who were invited without the mark of the McAllister brand stamped on their fore or hind-heads. But Miss Nilsson was a prima donna immaculata, *with a record of indifference to many beauties, and therefore not dangerous to the morals of gilded dukedom, and Mr. Kalisch had many recommendable qualities to secure him a friendly reception in society. He could crawl on his knees or dance on his hind legs and lick hands, like a small Chihuahua pet, if ordered by his wife Lilly; he could sing at receptions German ballads with a voice resembling the howl of a lovesick spitz if permitted by his wife Lilly; he could perform many feats, jump through a hoop into society, if pushed by his wife Lilly, or adorn the hall and parlors as a silent, motionless wall-flower, if put there by his wife Lilly. In fact, he was a charmingly little, and in every respect, perfect Lilly-put tenor.*[200]

The seasons of the opera from 1863 to 1867 were the most resplendent in the history of music in America, and the Academy of Music during that period was the temple of art and fashion, the rendezvous of intelligent refinement and elegance. There, during the entr'actes, grave statesmen discussed the burning questions of the day, while young ladies and gentlemen carried on their innocent flirtations.

---

[199] McAllister, a lawyer who lived in New York after 1852, was a leader in society and became arbiter of the city's social world.

[200] Paul Kalisch, German tenor, was married to German soprano, Lili Lehmann. Both frequently appeared together at the Met, following her debut there in 1885 (*Carmen*) and his in 1889. Lehmann's younger sister Marie was also a soprano (the two were no relation to Lotte). Both Lehmann and Kalisch withdrew after promising to sing in Maretzek's Golden Jubilee at the Met (1889). Speaking at the event, Maretzek importuned the audience to forgive Herr Kalisch, "the first artist I have ever known to give a true excuse. He said 'my wife won't let me sing,'" at which the house roared. A columnist speculated that the absences were related to Lehmann's rivalry with another soprano, Emma Fursch-Madi, who did perform in the benefit. *The American Musician*, 16 February 1889.

Nilsson, a Swedish soprano, starred in the first London performance of Thomas's *Mignon* (at Drury Lane, 1870) and re-created the role at New York's Academy of Music, 1871. She sang Marguerite in the opening production of *Faust* at New York's Metropolitan Opera in 1883.

There the musical student and the commercial clerk enjoyed their evenings in the family circle; there the Italian singing teachers frowned upon the Italian barbers when they gratefully applauded in the wrong place the tenor who had given them some free tickets. The possession of a private box was considered a sure sign of wealth and influence, and the splendor of feminine beauty eclipsed in the glamour of their sparkling diamonds. The manager too had been prosperous, had settled all shortcomings of former seasons and stocked the building of the Academy with full scores and orchestra, chorus, and solo parts of about one hundred operas, with a wardrobe of about ten thousand dresses, and with new scenery for twenty operas.

* * * *

Fire at the Academy. *In addition to the already great array of operatic artists, engagements for the next year had been already concluded with Sgr. Ronconi and with managers of Madame Parepa Rosa for her appearance in Italian opera, and everything seemed to point to the belief that Italian opera had been established on a firm basis, when on the morning of the 22nd of May 1866, I was early disturbed from my slumber in Staten Island by the unexpected arrival of Mr. Alfred Joel, my business manager, who handed me a morning paper with the following headings in large type: "The Great Fire: Total destruction of the Academy of Music—two firemen burned to death! $150,000 in music, wardrobes, and scenery destroyed" (fig. 14).*

The Academy had been underlet by me for a few nights to Mr. Jacob Grau, and, on the night of his production of Halevy's La Juive *with Madame Gazzaniga as the heroine, the audience had hardly left when the Academy was fired by incendiaries. My losses amounted to $60,000 (insurance: $10,000).*

The stockholders were insured for $150,000, and with the foundations intact and some of the walls still in good condition, the building could be replaced with $200,000. Therefore, my loss reached $50,000, while an assessment of $250 to each of the 200 stockholders was the extent of the damage to each of them. A meeting of the Board of Directors was held the following day and resolutions passed to rebuild the Academy at once, to be delivered to me on or before November 1 of the same year, whereupon I announced all my engagements with artists as holding and binding from November 1 next. Why the house could not be rebuilt with sufficient capital on hand within five months (from June to November), even allowing time for some pickings to those who controlled the rebuilding, remains a puzzling conundrum to this very day, but instead of 1 November 1866, the new Academy was put at my disposal on 1 March 1867, compelling me to travel around with an expensive opera company on hand during four months at a loss of about $10,000 per month!

Fig.14. **FIRE AT THE ACADEMY OF MUSIC,** New York, 21 May 1866, wood engraving, from Augustine Costello, *Our Firemen, A History of the New York Fire Departments* (New York: A. E. Costello, 1887)

As a compensation for the anxious and ruinous delay, I once more asked that the stockholders should retain their boxes and seats, but pay a nominal entrance fee or have free admissions and pay for their choice seats according to location. My demand was promptly met by an ironclad Lacedomonian phalanx of 200 stockholders, who were ready to fight and to die under the guidance of Leonidas (Henry Stebbins) for their sacred rights.

*   *   *   *

New York, Fall Season. Maretzek, always the indomitable, vowed that his fall season would proceed as planned. In addition to the celebrated buffo Giorgio Ronconi and his daughter, soprano Antoinetta, over the summer he engaged soprano Minnie Hauk and contralto Stella Bonheur. The company presented four performances in October at the Brooklyn Academy, featuring Ms. Hauk's debut in Bellini's *La sonnambula* and Ronconi's debut in the Riccis' *Crispino* (enticing New Yorkers across the river for a performance at which every seat was filled). The *Brooklyn Eagle* observed that Brooklyn had become "the 'operatic centre' of the Western hemisphere."[201] Following a brief season in Philadelphia and Pittsburgh, the company presented two additional performances at the Brooklyn Academy, during which Stella Bonheur made her debut as Siebel in Gounod's *Faust* and Mlle. Ronconi made her debut as Adina in Donizetti's *L'elisir d'amore*.

The company presented a season in Boston (November 12-25), performing en route in Hartford, before returning to New York to open at the Winter Garden (Mondays, Wednesdays, and Fridays, alternating with dramatic productions featuring the actor Edwin Booth on the remaining nights). The new opera of the season (first U.S. performance in Italian) was Hérold's *Zampa*, but it merited only three performances and an additional one the following spring. Despite the quality of the company, the season failed to meet expectations, and, as Maretzek noted, the cost of transporting a company from house to house proved exorbitant for its beleaguered manager.

The suit Maretzek had filed against the *Mercury Sun* at last came to trial on 18 December 1866. The transcript of the proceedings reveals that it was *Rigoletto* under attack for its morally-reprehensible plot (the scoundrel duke escapes punishment for his seduction of the virtuous Gilda, and she is brutally murdered by her unsuspecting father). Medori may have been the immoral artiste, since

---

[201] *Brooklyn Eagle*, 1 September 1866, p. 2.

she is the only singer mentioned, although the questioning was apparently limited to a discreet inquiry regarding her presence in the company. The verdict was reached in Maretzek's favor, and he was awarded $1,000 for damages.[202]

Italian opera, first heard in New York in the 1820s, had taken on increasing appeal for the aristocracy. They frequently were less interested in the opera itself than in its setting in a fashionable theater and in themselves seeing and being seen by other members of the audience. Unable to understand the language being sung or to follow the printed libretto, which often did not correspond to the cuts and interpolations made for a particular production,[203] audience members were wont to chat during performances, a habit that escalated as the century wore on. Jenny Lind's visit and her ability to communicate foreign texts may have encouraged society audiences wary of the language barrier to explore opera. Publicity that emphasized her youth, innocence, and virtue also appealed to their esteem for a high moral tone.

The influx at mid-century of immigrants from cultures where opera was a strong tradition and who became members of the working classes, however, led to inevitable conflicts with the aristocracy. These serious opera goers bitterly resented ornate chandeliers that blocked views from the least expensive seats (Astor Place), elaborate dress codes, private entrances, leased boxes, and difficulties in obtaining seats because of stockholder privileges (Academy of Music). The Astor Place Riot had been an outgrowth of some of these hostilities. The Academy was built in recognition of the desirability of making opera available to a wider audience. Its purpose as stated in its charter was to cultivate "a taste for music by concerts, operas, and other entertainments, which shall be accessible to the public at a moderate charge."[204]

1867

The company, Maretzek's "best . . . in many years," returned to Boston until late January and was back in New York for three performances at the Brooklyn Academy, preceding the reopening of the New York Academy of Music on

---

[202] New York (NY) Courts: Supreme Court, pp. 18, 45-51, 60.

[203] Preston, *Opera*, 170-71.

[204] Jay Robert Teran, "The New York Opera Audience, 1825-1974" (Ph.D. diss., New York University, 1974), 8, 16-27, 32; W.S.B. Mathews, *A Hundred Years of Music in America* (New York: AMS Press, 1970), 61-62.

March 7.[205] The *Tribune* declared Maretzek hero of a grand bal d'opera that
took place on March 1, with the theater placing second. The critic credits him
with having "done the best service in developing the lyric taste of this generation"
and observes that, without his "indomitable labors" New York would have had
no first-class opera at this time. He notes that, until 1860, "ruin was the normal
condition of operatic managers." An accompanying piece on the architecture
of the building judges it uglier than before, with more useless ornamentation,
and inferior to the excellent opera houses in Brooklyn and Boston.[206]

Maretzek described his company as a triple one, which could give twenty-
one standard operas without taxing the artists. Fanny Natali-Testa, contralto,
and Euphrosyne Parepa-Rosa, a Scottish soprano who had been singing in New
York since the previous October, joined the company in the spring. It was Parepa-
Rosa's first New York appearance in opera.[207] Maretzek also snared Angela
Peralta, nicknamed "the Mexican nightingale," who was en route from Havana
for a European tour. Peralta, the most prominent Mexican soprano of her era,
had auditioned for Sontag when the latter was in Mexico and had made her
debut in *Il trovatore* in Mexico City's Teatro Nacional at the age of fifteen.[208] On
April 3 the company premiered Petrella's *Il carnivale di Venezia*, which joined
L'Africana and *La stella del Nord* as the season's favorites.[209] Mazzoleni returned
to Italy at season's end.

*   *   *   *

Medori (April 1864). This gossipy narrative concludes "Further
Revelations":

*Madame Medori could have remained for many years the reigning operatic
favorite in New York, and she was disposed to make America her home, when
suddenly an incident in her life, in which she played the part of Norma in real life*

---

[205] *Brooklyn Eagle*, 18 February 1867, p. 2.

[206] *New York Tribune*, 2 March 1867, p. 5.

[207] Parepa returned to the stage in 1865, after the death of her first husband, for a concert tour to
the U.S. under H. L. Bateman. In 1867, she married Carl August Nicolas Rosa, violinist with the
Bateman Company, and later conductor and impresario. Brown, 2:73.

[208] R. Stevenson, 201-02. She and three members of her troupe died of yellow fever in Mazatlán,
Mexico, in 1883. *New York Times*, 9 September 1883, p. 7.

[209] *Brooklyn Eagle*, 23 April 1867, p. 1.

and off the stage, less successfully than on the boards of the Academy, prevented her further stay in this country. Madame Medori, shortly after her arrival in Havana, had received the sad news of her husband's death. Not that she would now, after the lapse of twelve months, renounce all earthly enjoyments and enter a convent for the rest of her life. On the contrary, she was yet in her best years, handsome, and of a sanguine temperament, but <u>virtuous</u>. She passed her evenings, when not occupied at the opera, alone, by the chimney fire, uneasy, mournful, like a woman who has loved once or who is on the eve of loving again (fig. 15).

She had been looking around among the sons of this free country, and one evening our Norma espied in the front seats of the orchestra a very good-looking gentleman of Herculean proportions and of lofty mien, who watched her every movement and only laid his opera glass down when the occasion allowed him to applaud with hands and feet and to vociferate "Brava!" in a stentorian voice. A mutual flirtation! A mutual introduction by mutual friends, a mutual avowal of love, a mutual kiss, and Madame Medori consented to become the wife of Mr. [Blank]man, the well-known handsome lawyer of New York. The somewhat corpulent widow now behaved and danced like a young girl, changed her sadness

Fig. 15.   GIUSEPPINA MEDORI,
photograph

Courtesy of the Library of Congress

into frolicsome hilarity, while the shrewd lawyer, here and there, asked for a retainer, or a refresher for the future husband, as a slight advance on their mutual bliss, and swore eternal love and fidelity at least three times per day to his fair bride.

They were both rich, but what did she care for worldly riches? She only dreamed of beatitude in his possession, but he, with one eye on her charms, had the other one on her money and, having ascertained the exact amount of her savings and of her salary of $3,500 in gold per month (at that time about $6,000 in greenbacks), drew up a legal marriage contract by which he managed her fortune; and in case of the death of one of the contracting parties, the surviving one should become the only heir. He asked Madame Medori to agree and sign the documents. The happy bride took the papers and cheerfully promised to execute them and to exchange them on the wedding day previous to the ceremony.

They had decided to marry quietly at the end of the operatic season, during the month of April 1864, to pass their honeymoon in Europe, and to return the following autumn and then resume their avocations. One evening (a few days only before the event) while in her parlor expecting the arrival of the future husband, a singular presentiment seized her, followed by a feverish state of alternating dejection and hopeful glee, one of those love trances, which lull you in the sweetest and bitterest of dreams. She was awakened from her reveries by her chamber-maid, who announced that Madame L (the fashionable dressmaker from Fifth Avenue) had sent her mate to try the new wedding and traveling dresses. The mention of new dresses usually dispels any gloomy thoughts with ladies, and Miss Juliette (a young blooming French girl) was immediately admitted into the parlor, and the mysteries of trying on dresses began without delay.

"This wedding dress fits like a kid glove, it is really bewitching," remarked Miss Juliette. "It needs no alterations and no stuffing, but this is not astonishing. Madame is so well shaped! Won't he be happy, your husband?"

Madame Medori did not answer but looked with satisfaction in the large mirror.

"Now let us try the traveling dress," continued Miss Juliette, and in taking off the white satin robe, ventured to say, "I am sure your husband is young yet handsome and has some good business?"

"Certainly," answered Madame Medori, "He is a lawyer and one of the hand-somest men in New York."

Miss Juliette, pale and trembling with emotion, stopped suddenly in the middle of the parlor, as if nailed to the floor, with the skirt of the traveling dress spread out between her hands.

"What is the matter, Juliette? You are pale! Don't you feel well?" inquired Madame Medori.

"Oh, nothing, Madame, I am subject to palpitations," she replied, and murmuring to herself, "Foolish idea! There are many handsome lawyers in New York," she proceeded to adjust the skirt of Madame Medori, who expressed her approval and asked for the bodice of the new dress.

When her beautiful right arm had slipped in one of the sleeves, Miss Juliette paused and took courage to ask whether the marriage was to be a secret one, and whether the name of her husband should not be divulged.

"It is no secret any longer. It is even the town gossip that Mr. [Blank]man is my future husband."

She had hardly pronounced the name when Juliette fell back in an armchair and, in doing so, tore the bodice in two, leaving one portion on Madame's shoulders and holding the other high in her hands, "Mr. [Blank]man, you said!" screamed Juliette, "Never!"

It was now Madame Medori's turn to tremble with fear and passion.

"Are you crazy, Juliette? Why never?"

"Because he loves me and only me," replied Juliette, stamping with her feet and tearing the remaining part of the bodice into shreds.

"I pity you, poor deluded girl, you would not think so if you had seen him on his knees yesterday at supper, swearing that he loved me with all his soul."

"And you would not be so sure, if you had heard him early this morning at breakfast swearing that he loves me with all his heart!"

"At breakfast! An early breakfast, you say?!" interrupted Madame Medori with fire in her eye. "What does this mean?"

Juliette, satisfied with the effect her words produced on her rival, became more calm and with as much heedless effrontery as ever a French modiste was capable of, she tauntingly answered, "Do you suppose I would let him go without breakfast?"

It was time for Madame now to swoon away on the sofa opposite, for the door was opened suddenly and before them stood Mr. [Blank]man himself, as large as life. He understood with one glance the situation, but he was not the kind of lawyer to be baffled by an unfortunate occurrence. He perceived that his matrimonial game was probably knocked as high as a kite, but he would not be beaten, only in case of necessity would he retreat in good order.

Smiling most lovingly at each of them, he at once invited their attack by remarking, "Are you rehearsing the first finale of Norma?"

In fact, there he stood defiantly, like the Roman pro-consul, but Medori, the grand Norma on the stage, had become the whimpering Adalgisa at home, while Juliette haughtily assumed the part of Norma.

"*You monster, you villain, you wretch! This lady pretends that only yesterday you swore to love her with all your soul. Can you deny it?*"

"*No, my dear,*" answered the lawyer, blandly, "*it is true.*"

Hardly had he admitted it when Madame Medori recovered from her fainting fit and, with a gleam of satisfaction in her eye, she said: "*And this milliner girl here claims that this morning you swore to love her with all your heart. It is false, is it not?*"

"*No, Madame,*" responded the lawyer cavalierly, "*I certainly did swear it. It is the truth and nothing but the truth.*"

"*What boldness! And you dare to confess it in the presence of both of us?*"

"*Let me explain, Madame,*" calmly pleaded the man of law with a persuasive smile on his lips. "*I did swear that I loved you with all my soul. Have I not a soul? Well, I love you with all my soul,*" and turning to Juliette, he said, "*I certainly swore that I loved you with all my heart! Have I not a heart? Well, I love you with all my heart!*"

"*This is going too far,*" exclaimed Medori. "*He is fooling us both!*"

Juliette continued at the highest pitch of her voice, "*Monstrous ogre! Villain, bluebeard, infamous traitor! I have sacrificed to you my honor, my life, and rejected the brilliant offers which Mr. B........, the banker of Broad Street is making me! And how do you repay my disinterested love? By trying to abandon me without notice and to run away clandestinely and with whom? Ha! Ha! With a theater princess, three times f: fair, fat, and forty!*"

Without waiting for a rejoinder, she rushed out of the house.

"*At last, we are alone,*" stammered Mr. [Blank]man, trying to catch the hands of Medori and to plead forgiveness, but she withdrew them brusquely, and, reaching a paper from her bureau, having regained her perfect composure, said disdainfully, "*This is our marriage contract. You see I have already signed and sealed it, but in this shape, I deliver it!*"

With these words, she tore the agreement to pieces, threw it at his feet, sailed majestically out of the parlor, and locked herself up in her boudoir.

Mr. [Blank]man concluded that the contemplated marriage, even if yet possible, would not be desirable without the contract and its stipulations and that it would be harder to make her again sign such an agreement than to obtain her pardon. He therefore placidly lighted a cigar, pressed his hat towards his right ear, kissed the chambermaid who just passed carrying smelling bottles and camphor to her mistress, and descended to the street peacefully.

Having disposed in his mind of Medori, he turned his attention to Juliette, and puffing his cigar, he soliloquized thus:

Juliette is a luscious bit of a girl, and it would be easy to
pacify her, but she will now probably prefer the offer of jewels,
dresses, and a well-furnished apartment from Mr. B..... to
my empty-handed love, or she will pretend the same liberality
from me. Bah! There are plenty of other girls but I ought
to have some kind of revenge for all this. Hallo! Has not
Mr. B....., the banker in question, a wife? Certainly, yes! And
a pretty one, too! That will do!

He lighted a fresh cigar and went joyfully home. Before a year had elapsed,
Mrs. B....., the banker's wife, obtained a divorce from her husband, and Mr.
[Blank]man had acted as her attorney!
Medori refused positively to renew her theatrical engagements in America,
renounced the stage, and returned to her home in Brussels. Her widowhood,
however, troubled her a great deal and proved an unbearable weight, which
depressed her mind and oppressed her poor heart, and finally she married a
fashionable tailor in Brussels. But that marriage was a misfit. The proverb says
that nine tailors make one man, and Madame Medori was certainly not the woman
to be happy with the ninth part of a man. She pined away, longing and sighing
for the fickle lawyer (who was every inch a man) until her death, which occurred
two years after her marriage with the sartorial artist.
Her last words, addressed to the beloved lawyer, were the pathetic ones from
Norma: "*Qual cor tradiste.*" [What a heart you betrayed.][210]

---

[210] *The New York Times* reported on 9 May 1864 that a new prima donna would be needed in the fall to replace Medori, "who, it is whispered by friends, and muttered by managers, has surrendered to the common enemy of the lyric stage—matrimony. The lady was, we believe, married last week to Mr. Blankman, the lawyer." The New York City marriage records for this period are illegible, but it seems dubious the marriage took place. Two Blankman brothers, Edmon and Benjamin, were practicing law in New York at this time. Edmon was better known, at least in part because of the sudden death in 1860 at age thirty-seven, under mysterious circumstances, of his first wife, a former "notorious courtesan," to whom he had been married for two years. A second post mortem ruled the cause of death as a stroke, but her will, leaving most of her substantial property holdings to her husband, was challenged as a forgery by her blood relatives. Edmon, in turn, charged that the relatives were brazen parasites preying on her wealth. The will was ruled as valid a year later.

Edmon, described in his obituary as "a prominent criminal lawyer," retired in 1865 following a second marriage. His wife, Annie, died the day after his own death of heart disease in 1895. They lived in a brownstone at 206 W. 123d St. (still extant), a few blocks from where Maretzek's great granddaughter was later to grow up. *New York Times*, 18 October 1860, p. 8; 19 October 1860, p. 8; 19 February 1861, p. 2; 23 September 1861, p. 8; 15 May 1895, p. 9.

Maretzek's version of Medori's demise is unfounded, since her death in 1906 followed his by nine years.

After 1867

Maretzek continued to manage opera in New York for several years after his account here terminates. He commented in an interview published in 1892 about the vogue for French *opéra bouffe* that pervaded the city in the 1860s, "It is impossible to prophesy anything about popular taste in New York. Popular taste is a fickle flirt. When, in 1868, after thirty years of exertions, we believed that the works of Rossini, Meyerbeer, Verdi and of other masters had taken a firm root in the taste of the public, there appeared on the west side of Fourteenth street the *Grand duchesse*, with French opera bouffe singers, and swept the love for legitimate opera away like a tidal wave, and nothing could stem the torrent but the importation of stars like Nilsson and Lucca."[211] (Pauline Lucca was Maretzek's prima donna for the 1872-73 season at the Academy.)[212] Maretzek made his Chicago debut in 1868, conducting all seven performances (February 3-8) of his troupe, combined with Leonard Grover's company, at Crosby's Opera House. His troupe also opened its season there the next fall (September 28-October 17), as negotiations for London impresario James Henry Mapleson to open in New York were collapsing, leaving the Academy of Music without tenants. Maretzek's seasons at the Academy ended in the early 1870s (fig. 16). His wife continued to perform there as harpist with the orchestra through the decade.

Mme Maretzek sold the 36-acre property they had purchased in 1865 five years later at a $4,000 profit, and Max Strakosch purchased the same property two years later, subsequently living there briefly. He eventually sold the house, but 34 acres remained in his estate at his death in 1892.[213] In the summer of 1869, Maretzek established a brick-making business, staffed by available tenors and baritones, on his Staten Island property that continued into at least the early 1870s.[214] Maretzek and Max Strakosch jointly managed a company that toured the country in 1872, co-starring Pauline Lucca and Clara Louise Kellogg (the Lucca-Kellogg Company).[215] In 1873-74, Maretzek presented brief seasons

---

[211] "Max's Memories," 94.

[212] Mme Lucca later filed suit against Maretzek for $15,000 in a London court for breach of contract. The judge ruled in Maretzek's favor. *New York Times*, 11 February 1878, p. 5.

[213] Richmond County Real Estate Records: Deeds, liber 84, p. 479; Robinson Atlas, 1898 (Topographical Records Office, Staten Island Borough Hall).

[214] *Brooklyn Eagle*, 13 August 1869, p. 3; *Spirit of the Times* 87, no. 20 (27 June 1874): 500.

[215] Oscar Thompson, *The American Singer: A Hundred Years of Success in Opera* (New York: Dial, 1937), 76.

**Fig. 16. MAX MARETZEK,
photograph by C. D. Fredericks**

Courtesy of the Dramatic Museum Archives,
Rare Book and Manuscript Library,
Columbia University, New York

at the Grand Opera House and the Lyceum, but was unable, even with Pauline Lucca and Ilma Di Murska, to pull audiences away from the Academy.[216] He sold the music for forty operas, together with his entire operatic wardrobe, to Maurice Grau the following summer.[217]

In (9, 10, 14) April 1875 Maretzek presented the U.S. premiere of Flotow's *L'ombre* (in Italian) at the Academy and in Brooklyn.[218] Reviews suggest that his insistence earlier in his career on achieving quality throughout his company had declined and that he now favored a star system, even though it meant working with inferior secondary singers and a less-accomplished orchestra and chorus. Through the 1870s he taught singing and continued to conduct and compose:

---

[216] Odell, 9:416. The Grand Opera House, originally known as Pike's Opera house, was erected by Samuel N. Pike at Twenty-third Street and Eighth Avenue in 1868. Demolished in 1960, it stood on property that had belonged to the estate of Clement C. Moore. The seating capacity was 1,883. The Lyceum Theatre was reconstructed from the former French Theatre under the direction of Charles Fechter, with financial backing from William Butler Duncan, a banker, and opened in 1873, shortly after Duncan and the former owner ejected Fechter in a rift over financing. Brown, 2:599, 461; *New York Times*, 27 March 1873, p. 5.

[217] *Spirit of the Times* 87, no. 20 (27 June 1874): 500.

[218] Odell, 9:594.

Baba, a play for which he wrote the music, was performed at Niblo's Garden in September 1876 with Maretzek conducting. Jacob Grau died the next year in New York after an illness of six years.[219]

Maretzek organized the Max Maretzek English Opera Company in the fall of 1879 for a short season at the Academy. His opera *Sleepy Hollow* or *The Headless Horseman,* based on the Washington Irving story, with a libretto by Charles Gayler, was included in the repertory (September 25-October 4).[220] Reviewers noted the work's indebtedness to earlier Italian models and found the quality of the company somewhat deficient. They commended its "pleasing melody," "pretty music," and its composer's "experienced eye for dramatic effect."[221] Audiences were initially attracted to the new work, but attendance languished, and a week at Brooklyn's Park Theatre also brought inadequate receipts.

The company left on November 10 for two weeks in Chicago, followed by performances in St. Louis. After a flurry of excitement surrounding the opening nights, audience attendance was sparse. Florence Rice Knox, the contralto with the company, attributes the new opera's tepid reception to a number of factors: the libretto, poor weather, inadequate publicity, timing (they followed the touring Strakosch opera company). She quotes a distraught Maretzek in Chicago, "I am ruined. There is nothing left for me to do. If I were only a young man I would not care so much, but I am an old man, and have failed." His wife, who had been a member of his company on earlier tours and might have helped to soothe his distress, was then on tour in New Orleans, as harpist with the Strakosch company.

By the time the company reached St. Louis in December, Maretzek was so mentally and physically exhausted, caused by disappointment and worry over finances, that he abruptly abandoned his company without notice and returned to New York alone. His action led to a frantic search for him in St. Louis and reports of his disappearance in the New York papers. His subsequent safe arrival in New York was sympathetically reported in articles recalling his contributions to the establishment of Italian opera.[222] Maretzek succeeded Theodore Thomas as musical director of the Cincinnati College of Music in September 1880, but resigned in

---

[219] *New York Times,* 17 December 1877, p. 8.

[220] For a full description of the work, see Deane L. Root, *American Popular Stage Music, 1860-1880* (Ann Arbor: UMI, 1981), 162-64.

[221] *New York Times,* 1 October 1879, p. 5; *New York Tribune,* 26 September 1879, p. 5; *Dwight's Journal of Music* 39 (6 December 1879): 199.

[222] *New York Times,* 7 December 1879, p. 7; 8 December 1879, p. 5; *New York Tribune,* 7 December 1879, p. 5; 9 December 1879, p. 5; 14 December 1879, p. 2.

March 1882, after a dispute with the college's president, Col. George Ward Nichols, also owner of a local pork-packing business. Theodore Thomas had withdrawn under similar circumstances. Mme Maretzek and their son also taught there.[223]

James Mapleson brought his London opera company from Her Majesty's Theatre and occupied the Academy for the 1878-79 season and for subsequent seasons through 1886. The Metropolitan Opera opened (with Gounod's *Faust*, in Italian) on 22 October 1883. Mme Maretzek played harp in the orchestra during that first season. Maretzek was honored on 12 February 1889 with a Golden Jubilee celebration at the Met in honor of the fiftieth anniversary of his debut conducting opera. Participants included Maude Powell, Anton Seidl, Theodore Thomas, Rafael Joseffy, and Walter Damrosch, in a program consisting chiefly of opera excerpts.[224] The Academy was unable to compete with the Met and closed its doors in 1886.

Maretzek conducted occasionally during his retirement, but made his living primarily as a vocal coach, commuting from Staten Island to his Manhattan studio at 40 W. Twenty-seventh Street. He taught at the New York Conservatory of Music (5 East Fourteenth Street), as well as its Brooklyn branch (102-6 Court Street) in the 1870s.[225] He read avidly and owned a large collection of autographs and inscribed photos.[226] *Sharps and Flats* was published in 1890. He suffered from heart disease (perhaps exacerbated by a predilection for cigars), and made fewer trips into the city near the end of his life. He died at age seventy-five on 14 May 1897, after a second stroke and an illness of about a month. An Episcopalian clergyman officiated at his funeral at the Maretzeks' Staten Island home. His obituaries credit him with introducing singers of the first rank, premiering a lengthy list of operas in the U.S., and being the "most noted promulgator of opera in this country for twenty years after the Academy opened." They note that, like most impresarios, he died a poor man.[227]

---

[223] *Dwight's Journal of Music* 40 (28 August 1880): 144; "Max and Madame Maretzek," *Cincinnati Enquirer*, 16 October 1881, p. 12; Krehbiel, *Chapters of Opera*, 55-56; *New York Times*, 11 March 1882, p. 1; 13 March 1882, p. 4; 14 March 1882, p. 5.

[224] *New York Times*, 3 February 1889, p. 9.

[225] *Brooklyn Eagle*, 24 September 1874, p. 1; 28 January 1877, p. 3.

[226] Jacobsen, 18; *New York Times*, 10 February 1889, p. 16. Maretzek stayed at his daughter Antoinette's home at 21 Fifth Ave. (at E. Ninth Street) just north of Washington Square Park, when he was in the city. She was married to Henry A. Lindsay, a stockbroker, amateur painter, and early member of the Salmagundi Club. *New York Tribune*, 7 December 1897, p. 1.

[227] *New York Times*, 15 May 1897, p. 7; *New York Tribune*, 15 May 1897, p. 7; *Brooklyn Eagle*, 15 May 1897, p. 6; E. S. Martin, "This Busy World," *Harpers Weekly* 41 (29 May 1897): 535; 10 July 1897,

Near the end of Maretzek's career as an impresario, the *Brooklyn Eagle* assessed his career, "if we judge his management by that of others who have essayed the difficulties of Italian Opera we must accord him the highest credit as an impressario [*sic*]. Maretzek has given the best performances of Italian Opera ever seen in New York or Brooklyn. He has kept faith with the public, and served them to the best of his ability on all occasions. That the Italian Opera has maintained any kind of footing at all in this country is due mainly to Maretzek. He has stuck to it indomitably under discouragements that had long since driven all other Opera Managers from the field."[228]

Nearly two decades later *The American Musician* saluted him: "The genial and universally beloved impresario has been a part of New York City since 1847, and his ceaseless activity has only been rivaled by that of the New York Post Office Department. Beside being the 'Napoleon of Impresarios,' a title conferred a quarter of a century ago upon him, he is a man of ideas and the truest friend the musical public ever had here. He found New York a ninth rate musical city, and with indomitable energy set to work to make it a first class center, and to do this he engaged the greatest talent here and abroad, standing up for American singers and musicians and giving them an equal show with his wonderfully chosen foreign artists. The true test of his judgment in selecting artists and distinguishing talent, even when ignored by others, is in fact that 90 per cent of the artists he engaged to sing for him during his long career were successes and became popular favorites. His companies were complete; there was no destructive star system. His contralto was always as good as his soprano, and his baritones were as fine as his tenors. Then he had a superb orchestra; scenery of the most sumptuous kind then known; the finest set of operatic choristers ever heard in New York. . . ."[229]

His wife, nearly blind, lived on until 1909, residing for a time in the San Francisco Bay Area with son, Max, and his wife, Marguerite (a former pupil of

---

p. 686; "The Progress of the World: The Month's Death Roll," *Review of Reviews* 15 (June 1897): 661; "Current History and Opinion: Max Maretzek," *The Chautauquan* 25 (July 1897): 423. Since Maretzek's will is not on file with the Richmond County Surrogate Court, it did not require probate. No evidence is to be found of substantial assets passed on to his children, who lived modestly, with the exception of his daughter Antoinette. She lived in Paris with her husband for several years after his retirement and left a significant estate (presumably acquired during his career as a stockbroker). At age eighty-eight, she was taken to Bellevue Hospital and was found to be wearing a silk money belt containing $128,525. Diagnosed with "senile psychosis," she spent her remaining years at Rockland State Hospital. "Last Will and Testament of Antoinette Maretzek Lindsay"; *New York Times*, 2 October 1948, p. 13; 3 October 1948, p. 67; 13 October 1948, p. 22.

[228] *Brooklyn Eagle*, 29 March 1869, p. 2.

[229] *The American Musician*, as reprinted, *Brooklyn Eagle*, 14 August 1887, p. 11.

Madame's), who both taught music in Oakland. She had returned to Mexico City in 1890 as harpist with the Abbey-Grau (Maurice) opera company, which also included Adelina Patti and Lillian Nordica.[230] The entire family, with the exception of son Max and his family, now lies buried within a few yards of one another in the Moravian Cemetery at New Dorp, Staten Island. The cemetery is nonsectarian, although a section on the south side of Todt Hill is designated for members of the United Brethren faith. A Vanderbilt mausoleum is located not far from the Maretzek plots.

Maurice Strakosch died in Paris in 1887 at age sixty-three, his wife, Amalia, in 1915. Max Strakosch was stricken with paralysis in his early fifties and died at age fifty-six (1892) in New York. Both Strakosch brothers apparently had the financial means to live comfortably in later years.[231]

Of the forty operas in the Maretzek company's repertory between 1862 and 1867, only *Don Giovanni* and the three Rossini operas had been premiered more than forty years earlier. The top ten operas, in order of popularity, were Gounod's *Faust* (by far the favorite), the Riccis' *Crispino e la comare*, Meyerbeer's *L'Africaine* (performed in Italian), Verdi's *Il trovatore*, Bellini's *Norma*, Petrella's *Jone*, Auber's *Fra Diavolo*, Mozart's *Don Giovanni*, Donizetti's *Don Sebastiano*, and Verdi's *Ernani*. About half the repertory in Maretzek's company is in the current (since 1960) repertory of the New York Metropolitan Opera Company (see Appendix 4). Approximately a quarter of the operas are now performed with about the same degree of frequency as by Maretzek's company in the 1860s. For example, *Faust, Il trovatore,* and *Don Giovanni* are still popular. Roughly a third have increased in number of performances, including *La traviata, Rigoletto, Il barbiere di Siviglia, Lucia di Lammermoor, Roméo et Juliette, L'elisir d'amore,* and *La forza del destino.* About an eighth of the operas, including *L'Africaine, Fra Diavolo, Roberto il diavolo,* and *Lucrezia Borgia,* have declined in number of performances, and nearly a third have never been performed at the Met. Verdi, except for *Aroldo* and *I due foscari,* is performed more and Meyerbeer less. Four works premiered (in the U.S.) by Maretzek are still among the twelve most performed Met operas: *La traviata, Rigoletto, Faust* (Maretzek premiered the Italian version), and *Il trovatore.*

The five-year period encompassing "Further Revelations" featured twelve U.S. premieres: Auber's *Fra Diavolo* in Italian (it had previously been performed in French, English, and German), Cagnoni's *Don Bucefalo*, Donizetti's *Don Sebastiano,* Gounod's *Faust* in Italian (the German version had been presented

---

[230] Olavarria y Ferrari, 2:1271.

[231] *New York Times*, 11 October 1887, p. 5; 15 December 1915, p. 15; 18 March 1892, p. 1.

in Philadelphia seven days earlier by another company), his *Romeo e Giulietta* (in Italian), Meyerbeer's *L'Africana*, Peri's *Giuditta*, Petrella's *Il carnivale di Venezia*, his *Jone*, the Riccis' *Crispino e la comare*, and Verdi's *Aroldo* and *La forza del destino*. Additional U.S. premieres that Maretzek presented during his New York career included Donizetti's *Maria di Rohan*, *Parisina*, Flotow's *L'ombre* (in Italian), Meyerbeer's *Le prophète* (in Italian), Verdi's *Attila*, *Don Carlos* (in Italian), *Luisa Miller* (in Italian), *I masnadieri*, *Rigoletto*, *La traviata*, and *Il trovatore*.

Of Verdi's operas written after 1845, Maretzek presented the U.S. premieres of virtually all, except the last three (*Aida*, *Otello*, and *Falstaff*), the French *Les vêpres siciliennes*, *Jerusalem* (the French version of his 1843 *I Lombardi alla prima crociata*), and the four less successful operas, *Il corsaro*, *La battaglia di Legnano*, *Stiffelo* (later revised as *Aroldo*), and *Simon Boccanegra* (not given in the U.S. until 1932). The first performance of a Verdi opera in New York took place in 1847.[232]

"Indomitable" is the adjective most frequently used to describe Maretzek by writers from his own time to the present. Other adjectives applied to him were "indefatigable," "imperious," "irrepressible," "ingenious," "intrepid," "devious," "persevering," "ebullient," "picturesque," "plucky," "unquenchable," "audacious," "amiable," "clever," and "turbulent." He was dubbed "Maretzek the Magnificent" and the "Napoleon of Opera," although he preferred a reviewer's appellation (intended as disparaging), "Don Quixote," regarding his own dedication to Italian opera as analogous to the persevering, energetic, and gallant knight's dedication to his Dulcinea.[233]

Clara Louise Kellogg described him in her memoirs as handsome, having a vivid and compelling personality, and noted that he was so obstinate "he simply did not know how to give up a project merely because it was impossible."[234] Minnie Hauk considered him the "most able and sympathetic" of all the conductors with whom she worked, "for he felt every phrase with the singer."[235] While he most assuredly made enemies in the highly competitive environment in which he worked, contemporaries frequently commented on his genial personality. It was undoubtedly his personal qualities of dedication to his art, determination, cleverness, practicality, perseverance, and resilience, as well as his human

---

[232] *I Lombardi* premiered on 3 March 1847.

[233] *C&Q*, 4-7.

[234] Kellogg, 40, 55.

[235] Hauk, 102-03.

relations and management skills that, combined with his musicianship (pianist, composer, conductor), made him a prevailing force (though by no means the only one) in Italian opera in New York for nearly thirty years.

After 1850, the expansion of the railroad, the growth of cities, and an infusion of capable, educated immigrants all contributed to the creation of a period of great mental vigor, conducive to the growth of a rich musical life in the United States. A number of elaborate opera houses were constructed, of which the New York Academy of Music was the best known.[236] Other impresarios active during this period and many touring companies left their marks. Maretzek was, however, active in New York over a longer time than any other opera manager. He was also, for many seasons, the manager of the principal season at the Academy of Music, the chief center for opera in the city, and was the first impresario to conduct his own performances. More than any other manager during the third quarter of the nineteenth century, he was instrumental in whetting and satiating the appetite of New York audiences for Italian opera in the years preceding the founding of the Metropolitan Opera. He was committed to making opera affordable to audiences from the working and middle classes, as well as the elite. His influence extended up and down the eastern seaboard, to Cuba, and Mexico, and indeed, throughout the U.S., through the influence that New York exerted on artistic taste in other cities.

---

[236] "The Era of National Expansion," *Grove's Dictionary of Music and Musicians: American Supplement* (Philadelphia: T. Presser, 1920), pp. 13-15.

Appendix 1

PERFORMANCES

Max Maretzek's Opera Companies
1863-67

NEW YORK AND BROOKLYN ACADEMIES OF MUSIC
(INCLUDING NEW YORK WINTER GARDEN THEATRE, FALL 1866)

1863

Spring, March 6-April 20, and Benefit

1. March 6, Fri., *Il trovatore*: Medori, Sulzer, Mazzoleni, Bellini: first U.S. appearances for all; also D. Coletti, Ficher, Muller
   March 7, Sat., 1 p.m., *Il trovatore* (same cast also)
2. March 9, Mon., *Un ballo in maschera*: Mlle Ortolani-Brignole's U.S. debut (the Page)
3. March 11, Wed., *Ernani*: Biacchi's U.S. debut (Silva)
4. March 13, Fri., *La traviata*
   March 14, Sat. matinee, *Ernani*
   No performance March 16, Mon. (*Norma* rescheduled: Medori indisposed)
5. March 18, Wed., *Un ballo in maschera* (substituted for *Norma*—Medori still ill): Guerrabella, Bellini
   March 19, Bklyn. Thurs., *La traviata*
6. March 20, Fri., *La favorita*
   March 21, Sat., 1 p.m., *Un ballo in maschera*
7. March 23, Mon., *Norma*: Medori
8. March 25, Wed., *Linda di Chaminoux*: Sgr Minetti's U.S. debut (Carlo)
   March 26, Bklyn. Thurs., *Un ballo in maschera*
9. March 27, Fri., *Norma*: Medori
   March 28, Sat., 1 p.m., *La traviata*
10. March 30, Mon., *Semiramide*: Minetti's second appearance
11. March 31, Tues., *Lucia di Lammermoor*

12. April 1, Wed., *Norma*
    No performance Thursday or Friday (Good Friday)
    April 4, Sat. matinee, *Linda di Chamounix*; also 1st act, *Masaniello*
13. April 6, Mon., *Jone* (U.S. premiere; cast: see Kaufman,* p. 202)
14. April 8, Wed., *Jone*
15. April 9, Thurs. (NY), *Fidelio* (presented by Maretzek, but performed by German Opera Co.)
16. April 10, Fri., *Jone*
    April 11, Sat. matinee, *Lucia di Lammermoor*; also duet scene from *Puritani*
17. April 11, Sat. evening, *Martha* (presented by Maretzek, but performed by German Opera Co.)
18. April 13, Mon., *Jone*
19. April 15, Wed., *I due Foscari* (Maretzek benefit; cast: see Kaufman, p. 316)
20. April 17, Fri., *Norma*: Medori's farewell performance
    April 18, Sat., *Il barbiere di Siviglia*; also last scene, *Il trovatore*
21. April 20, Mon., *Un ballo in maschera* (Mazzoleni benefit); also new scene, *The Garibaldian*, composed for him by Pasani
    April 29, *Il trovatore* (Ferdinand Palma benefit)

Summer, May 4-18, and Benefit
6 performances announced, plus extra on May 18

22. May 4, Mon., Verdi's *Aroldo* (U.S. premiere; cast: see Kaufman, p. 464)
    No performance Tuesday (benefit at the Academy)
23. May 6, Wed., *Aroldo*
24. May 8, Fri., *Ernani*
    May 9, Sat., 1 p.m., *Aroldo*
25. May 11, Mon., *Il trovatore*: debut of Miss Parker (Leonora)
26. May 13, Wed., *Jone* (Guerrabella)
27. May 15, Fri., *Aroldo*
    May 16, Sat. matinee, *Jone* (*Giuditta* had been announced)
28. May 18, Mon. (extra performance), *Jone*
    May 23, Sat. matinee, *Jone*; also 4th act, *Rigoletto* (Bellini benefit)

Fall, October 5-November 28, and Benefit; December 23-30
Regular nights: Mon., Wed., Fri., Sat. matinee

1st series:

1. October 5, Mon., *Roberto Devereux*
2. October 7, Wed., *Roberto Devereux*

---

* Kaufman, *Verdi and His Major Contemporaries* (New York: Garland, 1990).

3. October 9, Fri., *Rigoletto* (with Kellogg)
   October 10, Sat. evening (extra night), *Norma* (with Medori)
4. October 12, Mon., *Norma* (*Ernani* had been announced, but not performed because of Mazzoleni's illness)
5. October 14, Wed., *Jone* (cast: see Kaufman, p. 203)
   October 15, Bklyn. Thurs., *Rigoletto* (with Kellogg)
6. October 16, Fri., *La traviata* (*Martha* announced)
   October 17, Sat. matinee, *Rigoletto*
7. October 19, Mon., *Ernani* (*Macbeth* had been announced, but postponed)
8. October 21, Wed., *Macbeth* (with Medori; cast: see Kaufman, p. 347)
   October 22, Bklyn. Thurs., *La traviata*
9. October 23, Fri., *Martha* (with Kellogg)
   October 24, Sat. evening, *Jone* (2nd grand extra night)
10. October 26, Mon., *Macbeth*
11. October 28, Wed., *Il trovatore*
    October 29, Bklyn. Thurs., *Martha*
12. October 30, Fri., *Jone*

2nd series:

October 31, Sat. matinee, *La traviata*
13. November 2, Mon., *Lucrezia Borgia*
14. November 4, Wed., *Lucrezia Borgia*
    November 5, Bklyn. Thurs., *Lucia di Lammermoor*
15. November 6, Fri., *Martha*
    November 7, Sat. matinee, *Lucia di Lammermoor*; also 2nd act, *Martha*
16. November 9, Mon., *Norma*
17. November 11, Wed., *Giuditta* (U.S. premiere; Havana premiere: 8 February 1863; casts: see Kaufman, pp. 176-77)
    November 12, Bklyn. Thurs., *Ernani*
18. November 13, Fri., *La sonnambula*
    November 14, Sat. evening, *Giuditta* (3rd grand extra night) (*Lucrezia Borgia* announced)
19. November 16, Mon., *Il trovatore*
    November 17, Tues., *Martha* and selections from *Semiramide* (proceeds for Hebrew Asylum for the Aged and Infirm)
20. November 18, Wed., *Jone*
21. November 20, Fri., *Don Giovanni*
    November 21, Sat. evening, *Lucrezia Borgia* (with Virginia Lorini) (4th grand extra night)
22. November 23, Mon., *Don Giovanni*
23. November 25, Wed., *Faust* (U.S. premiere in Italian)
    November 26, Thurs. (Thanksgiving, last grand extra night), *Macbeth* (Medori's last appearance of season)

24. November 27, Fri., *Faust*
    November 28, Sat. matinee, *La sonnambula*; also grand arias: *Semiramide* and *Lucia di Lammermoor*
    November 28, Bklyn. Sat. evening, *Norma*
    November 30, Mon., *Faust* (Maretzek benefit)
    December 23, Wed., *Un ballo in maschera*
    December 25, Fri., *Faust*
    December 26, Sat. matinee, *Don Giovanni*
    December 28, Mon., *Jone*
    December 30, Wed., *Faust*

1864

Winter, February 1-29, March 1-12
16 regular nights: Mon., Wed., Thurs., Fri., Sat. matinee

1. February 1, Mon., *Il trovatore* (*Jone* announced, but Biacchi was ill)
2. February 3, Wed., *Don Giovanni* (with Kellogg, Medori, Stockton, Lotti, Bellini, Biacchi)
3. February 4, Thurs., *Faust* (with Kellogg)
4. February 5, Fri., *I due Foscari* (with Medori)
   February 6, Sat. matinee, *Martha*
5. February 8, Mon., *Norma* (with Medori)
6. February 9, Tues., *Faust*
   No performance February 10, Ash Wed.
   February 11, Bklyn. Thurs., *Norma* (Arion Society ball at N.Y. Academy)
7. February 12, Fri., *Faust*
8. February 13, Sat. evening, *Jone*
9. February 15, Mon., *Un ballo in maschera*
10. February 17, Wed., *Poliuto* (revival)
11. February 19, Fri., *Faust* (by universal demand)
    February 20, Sat. matinee, *Norma*
12. February 22, Mon., *I puritani*: first appearance of Brignoli
13. February 24, Wed., *Jone*
14. February 25, Thurs., *La sonnambula*: 2nd night with Brignoli; indisposed for 3rd act
15. February 26, Fri., *Lucia di Lammermoor*: debut of Laura Harris
    February 27, Sat. evening (extra night), *Faust*
16. February 29, Mon., *Il trovatore*

Short season of 7 extra nights:

17. March 1, Tues., *Lucia di Lammermoor* (*Faust* had been scheduled; Kellogg indisposed)
18. March 2, Wed., *Macbeth*

19. March 4, Fri., *Lucrezia Borgia*
    March 5, Sat. matinee, *Faust* (Kellogg indisposed; her role sung in German)
20. March 7, Mon., *Ernani*
21. March 8, Tues., *Faust*
22. March 9, Wed., *Don Giovanni*
23. March 11, Fri., *Faust* (Biacchi ill; Mr. Herrmanns (Anschütz Co.) substituted: sang in German)
    March 12, Sat. matinee, *Faust* (abbreviated version)

Spring, March 28-April 18, and Benefits
Regular nights: Mon., Wed., Thurs., Fri., Sat. matinee

1. March 28, Mon., *Faust*
2. March 30, Wed., *Martha*
3. March 31, Thurs., *Faust*
4. April 1, Fri., *Roberto il diavolo*
   April 2, Sat. matinee, *Faust*
5. April 4, Mon., *Roberto il diavolo*
6. April 5, Tues., *Faust*
7. April 6, Wed., *Lucrezia Borgia*
   April 7, Bklyn. Thurs., *Lucia di Lammermoor* (Brignoli's first appearance of the season)
8. April 8, Fri., *Faust*
   April 9, Sat., *Jone* (Mazzoleni benefit) (grand extra night)
   April 11, Mon., *Roberto il diavolo*
   April 13, Wed., *Faust*
   April 14, Thurs., *Roberto il diavolo*
   April 15, Fri., *Faust*
   April 16, Sat. matinee, *Roberto il diavolo*
   April 18, Mon., *Faust* (31st performance and end of season)
   April 19, Bklyn. Tues., *Roberto il diavolo*
   April 20, Wed., *Faust* (Bellini benefit)
   April 21, Thurs., *La traviata*; also 2nd act, *Un ballo in maschera* (Ortolani-Brignole benefit)
   April 22, Fri., *Faust* (Sulzer benefit)
   April 23, Sat. matinee, *La sonnambula*, plus other selections in honor of 300th anniversary of Shakespeare's death (substituted for Nicolai's *Merry Wives of Windsor*, because of Mr. Hermanns's illness)

Fall, October 3-November 5
18 regular nights: Mon., Tues., Wed., Fri., and occasional Sat. matinees

1. October 3, Mon., *Il trovatore* (with Carozzi-Zucchi and Massimiliani; also his debut)

2. October 4, Tues., *La traviata*: Brambilla's debut
3. October 5, Wed., *Lucrezia Borgia* (with Carozzi-Zucchi and Susini)
   October 6, Bklyn. Thurs., *Il trovatore*
4. October 7, Fri., *Lucia di Lammermoor* (with Harris, Lotti)
   No Saturday matinee
5. October 10, Mon., *Il trovatore*
6. October 12, Wed., *Un ballo in maschera*
7. October 14, Fri., *Lucrezia Borgia* (*Faust* was announced)
   October 15, Sat., 1st grand matinee, *La traviata*
   October 15, Bklyn. Sat. evening, *Lucrezia Borgia*
8. October 17, Mon., *Faust* (with Kellogg, her first appearance of the season)
9. October 18, Tues., *Un ballo in maschera*
10. October 19, Wed., *Faust*
11. October 21, Fri., *Poliuto*
    No Saturday matinee
    October 22, Bklyn. Sat. evening, *Faust* (with Kellogg)
12. October 24, Mon., *Martha*
13. October 25, Tues., *Poliuto*
14. October 26, Wed., *Faust*
    October 27, Bklyn. Thurs., *Poliuto*
15. October 28, Fri., *Poliuto*
    October 29, Sat. matinee, *Faust*
16. October 31, Mon., *Il trovatore*
17. November 2, Wed., *Don Giovanni*
    November 3, Bklyn. Thurs., *Don Giovanni*
18. November 4, Fri., *Rigoletto*: Jennie Van Zandt's debut (Gilda)
    November 5, Sat. matinee, *Lucrezia Borgia*

(Fall)-Winter (2nd series), November 14-December 26, and Benefits

18 nights, plus extra nights and matinees

1. November 14, Mon., *Poliuto* (*Don Sebastiano* was announced—will be produced in a few days)
2. November 15, Tues., *Linda di Chamounix*
3. November 16, Wed., *Don Giovanni*
4. November 18, Fri., *Faust*
   No Saturday matinee
   November 19, Bklyn. Sat. evening, *Rigoletto* (with Van Zandt)
5. November 21, Mon., *Don Giovanni*
6. November 22, Tues., *Rigoletto*
7. November 23, Wed., *Martha*
8. November 25, Fri., 7:30, *Don Sebastiano* (U.S. premiere)

November 26, Sat. matinee, *Faust*
November 26, Bklyn. Sat. evening, *Poliuto*
9. November 28, Mon., *Don Sebastiano*
10. November 29, Tues., *Don Sebastiano*
11. November 30, Wed., *Faust*
12. December 2, Fri., *Don Sebastiano*
  December 3, Bklyn. Sat. evening, *Don Sebastiano*
13. December 5, Mon., *La figlia del reggimento*
14. December 6, Tues., *Don Sebastiano*
15. December 7, Wed., *Poliuto*
  December 8, Bklyn. Thurs., *Faust*
16. December 9, Fri., *Don Sebastiano*
  December 10, Sat. matinee, *La figlia del reggimento*
17. December 12, Mon., *Il trovatore*
  No opera Tuesday; Academy needed to rehearse *Fra Diavolo*
18. December 14, Wed., *Don Sebastiano*
  December 15, Bklyn. Thurs., *Don Giovanni*

Extra performances to produce *Fra Diavolo*:

19. December 16, Fri., *Faust*
  December 17, Sat. matinee, *Don Sebastiano*
20. December 19, Mon., *Don Sebastiano*
  No performance Tuesday
21. December 21, Wed., *Fra Diavolo* (U.S. premiere, Italian version)
  December 22, Bklyn. Thurs., *Don Sebastiano*
22. December 23, Fri., *Fra Diavolo*
  December 24, Sat. matinee, *Don Sebastiano*
23. December 26, Mon., *Fra Diavolo*
  December 27, Tues., *Norma* (Carozzi-Zucchi's benefit)
  December 28, Wed., *Fra Diavolo* (Kellogg's benefit, her first in N.Y.)
  December 29, Thurs., *Fra Diavolo* (benefit: French Benevolent Society)
24. December 30, Fri., *Norma*

1865

Spring, February 2-March 23, and Benefits
24 regular nights

1. February 2, Thurs., *Don Sebastiano*
2. February 3, Fri., *Fra Diavolo*
  February 4, Sat. matinee, *Poliuto*

3. February 6, Mon., *Il trovatore*
4. February 7, Tues., *Faust*
5. February 8, Wed., *Norma*
   February 9, Bklyn. Thurs., *Fra Diavolo*
6. February 10, Fri., *La traviata*
   No Saturday matinee
7. February 13, Mon., *Faust* (*Ernani* was announced, but Carozzi-Zucchi was ill)
8. February 14, Tues., *Fra Diavolo*
9. February 15, Wed., *Lucia di Lammermoor*
   February 16, Bklyn. Thurs., *Norma*
10. February 17, Fri., *Ernani*
    February 18, Sat. matinee, *Lucia di Lammermoor* (*Fra Diavolo* was announced, but Kellogg indisposed)
11. February 20, Mon., *Don Sebastiano*
12. February 21, Tues., *Martha*
13. No performance February 22, Wed., *Ernani* cancelled to prepare for *La forza del destino*
    February 23, Bklyn. Thurs., *Martha*
14. February 24, Fri., *La forza del destino* (U.S. premiere; cast: see Kaufman, p. 484)
    No Saturday matinee
    February 25, Bklyn. Sat. evening, *Linda di Chamounix*
    February 27, Bklyn. Mon., *Ernani* (Carozzi-Zucchi's benefit, her first U.S.)
15. February 28, Tues., *La forza del destino*
16. March 1, Wed., *La sonnambula*
    March 2, Bklyn. Thurs., *La figlia del reggimento*
17. March 3, Fri., *La forza del destino*
    March 4, Sat. matinee, *Martha* (*Fra Diavolo* was announced, but proved "impractical")
18. March 6, Mon., *La forza del destino*
19. March 7, Tues., *Faust*
20. March 8, Wed., *La forza del destino*
    March 9, Bklyn. Thurs., *Faust*
21. March 10, Fri., *La forza del destino*
    March 11, Sat. matinee, *Ernani*
    March 11, Bklyn. Sat. evening, *Linda di Chamounix* (Kellogg benefit)
22. March 13, Mon., *Don Giovanni*
    March 14, Bklyn. Tues., *La forza del destino*
23. March 15, Wed., *Fra Diavolo*
    March 16, Thurs., *Norma* (not in Bklyn.)
    March 17, Fri., *I puritani*
    March 18, Sat. matinee, *La forza del destino*
    March 20, Mon., *La figlia del reggimento*; also 4th act, *Rigoletto*
    March 21, Tues., *Don Sebastiano*

March 22, Bklyn. Wed., *Don Giovanni*
March 23, Thurs. matinee, *Fra Diavolo*
April 10, Bklyn. Mon., *I puritani* (Maretzek benefit at Brooklyn Academy of Music)
April 11, Tues., *Poliuto*; also 3rd act, *La forza del destino* and other misc. (Maretzek benefit)

Fall, September 25-December 16
20 regular nights (2 series): Mon., Tues., Wed., Fri.

1st series:

1. September 25, Mon., *Faust*: debuts of Irfrè and Antonucci
   No performance Tuesday
2. September 27, Wed., *Poliuto*
   September 28, Bklyn. Thurs., *Faust*
3. September 29, Fri., *Lucrezia Borgia*
   September 30, Sat. matinee, *Faust*
4. October 2, Mon., *Jone*: E. Bosio debut (cast: see Kaufman, p. 203)
5. October 3, Tues., *Jone*
6. October 4, Wed., *Ernani*: Marra's debut (new baritone)
   October 5, Bklyn. Thurs., *Jone*
7. October 6, Fri., *Un ballo in maschera*
   No Saturday matinee
8. October 9, Mon., *Il trovatore*: Mlle. B. de Rossi's debut (Azucena)
9. October 10, Tues., *I puritani*
10. October 11, Wed., *Ernani*
    October 12, Bklyn. Thurs., *Poliuto*
11. October 13, Fri., *Martha*
    October 14, Sat. matinee, *Jone*
12. October 16, Mon., *La traviata*
13. October 17, Tues., *Lucrezia Borgia* (combined with a concert by the Bateman Co.)
14. October 18, Wed., *Lucia di Lammermoor* (followed another Bateman Co. concert)
    October 19, Bklyn. Thurs., *Martha*
15. October 20, Fri., *Norma*
    No Saturday matinee
16. October 23, Mon., *Il trovatore* (*Crispino e la comare* was announced)
17. October 24, Tues., *Crispino e la comare* (U.S. premiere; Kellogg; also Rovere debut)
18. October 25, Wed., *Crispino e la comare*
    October 26, Bklyn. Thurs., *Norma*
19. October 27, Fri., *Crispino e la comare*
    October 28, Sat. matinee, *Ernani*
20. October 30, Mon., *Un ballo in maschera*

2nd series:

1. October 31, Tues., *Crispino e la comare*
2. November 1, Wed., *Jone* (Mazzoleni benefit)
   November 2, Bklyn. Thurs., *Crispino e la comare*
3. November 3, Fri., *Roberto il diavolo*
   November 4, Sat. matinee, *Crispino e la comare*
4. November 6, Mon., *Roberto il diavolo*
5. November 7, Tues., *Crispino e la comare*
6. November 8, Wed., *Rigoletto*
   November 9, Bklyn. Thurs., *Roberto il diavolo*
7. November 10, Fri., *Fra Diavolo*
   November 11, Sat. matinee, *Crispino e la comare*
   November 11, Sat. evening (extra performance), *Ernani*
8. November 13, Mon., *Crispino e la comare*
9. November 14, Tues., *Norma*
10. November 15, Wed., *Fra Diavolo* (General Grant attended)
    November 16, Bklyn. Thurs., *Ernani*
11. November 17, Fri., *Il trovatore*
    No Saturday matinee
    November 18, Bklyn. Sat. evening (extra night), *Crispino e la comare*
12. November 20, Mon., *Don Giovanni* (Rovere as Leporello for first time)
13. November 21, Tues., *Crispino e la comare*
14. November 22, Wed., *Ernani*
    November 23, Bklyn. Thurs., *Fra Diavolo*
15. November 24, Fri., *La sonnambula* (Ortolani benefit)
    November 25, Sat. matinee, *Fra Diavolo*
16. November 27, Mon., *Crispino e la comare*
    No performance Tuesday (needed to rehearse for *L'Africana*)
17. November 29, Wed., *Faust*
18. December 1, Fri., 7:30, *L'Africana* (U.S. premiere)
    December 2, Sat. evening (extra night), *L'Africana*
19. December 4, Mon., *L'Africana*
20. December 5, Tues., *Martha*
21. December 6, Wed., *L'Africana*
    December 7, Bklyn. Thurs., *Crispino e la comare*
22. December 8, Fri., *L'Africana*
    December 9, Sat. matinee, *L'Africana*
    December 9, Sat. evening, *Crispino e la comare*; 3rd act, *Roberto il diavolo*
       (benefit: French Benevolent Society)
24. December 11, Mon., *L'Africana*
25. December 12, Tues., *L'Africana*

26. No performance December 13, Wed., because of Rovere's death (*Crispino e la comare* originally scheduled, and *I puritani* announced as substitution because of his illness)

    December 14, Bklyn. Thurs., *L'Africana*
27. December 15, Fri., *L'Africana*

    December 16, Sat. matinee, *L'Africana* (hundreds had been unable to gain admittance at December 9 matinee)

1866

Spring, February 1-April 14, and Benefits

1. February 1, Thurs., *L'Africana*
2. February 2, Fri., *Crispino e la comare*

   February 3, Sat. matinee, *Norma*
3. February 5, Mon., *I puritani*
4. February 6, Tues., *L'Africana*
5. February 7, Wed., *Faust*

   February 8, Bklyn. Thurs., *L'Africana*
6. February 9, Fri., *L'Africana*

   February 10, Sat., *Crispino e la comare* (11 a.m., because of Philharmonic rehearsal)
7. February 12, Mon., *Martha*
8. February 13, Tues., *Don Sebastiano*
9. February 14, Wed., *Don Sebastiano*

   February 15, Bklyn. Thurs., *Crispino e la comare*
10. February 16, Fri., *Fra Diavolo*

    February 17, Sat. matinee, *Ernani*: debut of Sgr Brandini, baritone (Don Carlos)
11. February 19, Mon., *L'Africana*
12. February 20, Tues., *Crispino e la comare*
13. February 21, Wed., *Poliuto* (*Don Pasquale* announced; debut of Brandini—not sufficiently rehearsed)

    February 22, Bklyn. Thurs., *La sonnambula*
14. February 23, Fri., *Don Sebastiano*

    February 24, Sat. matinee, 11 a.m., *Jone*
15. February 26, Mon., *La favorita*: debut of C. Poch (Leonora)
16. February 27, Tues., *L'Africana*
17. February 28, Wed., *La sonnambula*

    March 1, Bklyn. Thurs., *Don Sebastiano*
18. March 2, Fri., *La favorita* (Poch's 2nd appearance)

    March 3, Sat. matinee, *Don Pasquale*: Sarti debut

    (Tuesday no longer a regular night; to be set aside for benefits of the leading artists)

19. March 5, Mon., *Il trovatore*
    March 6, Tues., *L'Africana* (Mazzoleni benefit)
20. March 7, Wed., *Don Pasquale*
    March 8, Bklyn. Thurs., *Il trovatore*
21. March 9, Fri., *La stella del Nord* (with Kellogg; revival: introduced by Maretzek ten
    years ago)
    March 10, Sat. matinee, *La favorita* (last appearance of C. Poch)
22. March 12, Mon., *La stella del Nord*
    March 13, Tues. (extra night), *L'Africana* (Carozzi-Zucchi benefit)
23. March 14, Wed., *La stella del Nord*
    March 15, Bklyn. Thurs., *La stella del Nord*
24. March 16, Fri., *Un ballo in maschera*
    March 17, Sat. matinee, *La stella del Nord*
    March 17, Bklyn. Sat. evening, *L'Africana* (Carozzi-Zucchi benefit)

Benefits and extra performances:

    March 19, Mon., *Jone* (E. Bosio benefit; her first in the U.S.)
    March 20, Tues., *L'Africana* (Bellini benefit)
    March 21, Wed., *La stella del Nord* cancelled: Kellogg ill (was to have been her benefit)
    March 22, Bklyn. Thurs., *Don Giovanni* (Bellini benefit)
    No performance March 23, Fri., *Norma* cancelled; Massimiliani benefit had been
        announced: all artists needed for *Don Giovanni* on Saturday
    March 24, Sat. matinee, 11 a.m., *Don Giovanni*
    March 26, Mon., *La stella del Nord* (Kellogg benefit—rescheduled from March 21)
    March 31, Sat. matinee, *Faust*
    March 31, Sat. evening, *L'Africana*
    April 2, Mon., *Gli Ugonotti* (revival)
    April 3, Tues., *Gli Ugonotti*
    April 4, Wed. matinee, *Crispino e la comare*
    April 4, Wed. evening, *Lucrezia Borgia* (with C. Poch)
    April 5, Thurs., bal d'opera
    April 6, Fri., *Fra Diavolo*
    April 7, Sat., 11 a.m., *Lucrezia Borgia*
    April 7, Bklyn. Sat. evening, *Gli Ugonotti*
    April 9, Mon., *Gli Ugonotti*
    April 10, Tues., *Martha*
    April 11, Wed., *La favorita* (with C. Poch) (*Norma* was announced, but Carozzi-
        Zucchi was ill)
    April 12, Bklyn. Thurs., *Fra Diavolo* (Kellogg benefit)
    April 13, Fri., *La stella del Nord*
    April 14, Sat. matinee, *Gli Ugonotti*

Fall (after New York Academy fire), October 10-13, November 5-6, 26-December 28

Brooklyn Academy of Music

1. October 10, Wed., *Crispino e la comare* (with Ronconi)
2. October 11, Thurs., *Il trovatore*
3. October 12, Fri., *Fra Diavolo* (with Ronconi)
4. October 13, Sat. evening, *La sonnambula*: Hauk and Baragli debuts

Brooklyn Academy of Music

1. November 5, Mon., *Faust*: Stella Bonheur's debut (Siebel)
2. November 6, Tues., *L'elisir d'amore*: Mlle. Ronconi's debut

Winter Garden Theatre, unless otherwise noted (alternating with Edwin Booth); opera nights: Mon., Wed., Fri.

1. November 26, Mon., *Crispino e la comare* (with Ronconi)
   November 27, Bklyn. Tues., *Ernani*
2. November 28, Wed., *Fra Diavolo*
   November 29, Bklyn. Thurs., *L'elisir d'amore*
3. November 30, Fri., *La stella del Nord*: Minnie Hauk N.Y. debut (Prascovia)
   December 1, Sat. matinee, *Il trovatore*
4. December 3, Mon., *La stella del Nord*
5. December 5, Wed., *Gli Ugonotti*
   December 6, Bklyn. Thurs., *La stella del Nord*
6. December 7, Fri., *Faust*
   December 8, Sat. matinee, *Lucrezia Borgia*
7. December 10, Mon., *Crispino e la comare*
8. December 12, Wed., *Il barbiere di Siviglia*
   December 13, Bklyn. Thurs., *Il barbiere di Siviglia*
9. December 14, Fri., *Il trovatore*
   December 15, Sat. matinee, *Fra Diavolo*
10. December 17, Mon., *Zampa* (Italian version with recitatives)
    December 18, Bklyn. Tues., *Crispino e la comare*
11. December 19, Wed., *Zampa*
    December 20, Bklyn. Thurs., *Zampa*
12. December 21, Fri., *La sonnambula* (Hauk as Amina for 1st time)
    December 22, Sat. matinee, *Faust*
13. December 24, Mon., *Crispino e la comare*
14. December 26, Wed., *Un ballo in maschera*: Miss McCulloch's debut
15. December 28, Fri., *Il barbiere di Siviglia*

1867

Spring, March 7-April 30, and Benefits
30 regular nights at New York Academy

January 31, Bklyn. Thurs., *Fra Diavolo*

February 14, Bklyn. Thurs., *Il barbiere di Siviglia*

February 28, Bklyn. Thurs., *Martha*

March 1, grand bal d'opera for reopening of N.Y. Academy: in honor of and as benefit for Maretzek

March 2, Sat. p.m., inaugural matinee (excerpts)

March 5, Bklyn. Tues., *Martha*

1. March 7, Thurs., *Il barbiere di Siviglia* (with Kellogg as Rosina): grand opening of N.Y. Academy

2. March 8, Fri., *Fra Diavolo*

March 9, Sat. matinee, *Lucrezia Borgia* (with C. Poch) (*La sonnambula* had been announced; Hauk was ill)

3. March 11, Mon., *La stella del Nord*

4. March 12, Tues., *La favorita*

5. March 13, Wed., *Faust*

March 14, Bklyn. Thurs., *Don Pasquale* (with Hauk)

6. March 15, Fri., *Crispino e la comare*

March 16, Sat. matinee, *La favorita*; also 2nd act, *L'elisir d'amore* (with Mlle Ronconi) and dramatic readings

7. March 18, Mon., *Il trovatore*: opera debut of Parepa-Rosa (Leonora)

8. March 19, Tues., *Norma* (with Parepa-Rosa) (General Grant was present)

9. March 20, Wed., *La stella del Nord* (with Kellogg and Hauk)

March 21, Bklyn. Thurs., *Norma* (with Parepa-Rosa)

10. March 22, Fri., *Martha*

March 23, Sat. matinee, *Norma* (with Parepa-Rosa)

11. March 25, Mon., *Lucia di Lammermoor* (with Parepa-Rosa and Mazzoleni)

12. March 26, Tues., *Don Giovanni* (with Parepa-Rosa as Donna Anna)

No performance on Wednesday (Arion Society ball at the N.Y. Academy)

March 28, Bklyn. Thurs., *Don Giovanni* (with Parepa-Rosa)

13. March 29, Fri., *Don Giovanni* (Parepa-Rosa's last night)

March 30, Sat. matinee, *Il trovatore* (Parepa-Rosa's farewell matinee)

14. April 1, Mon., *Ernani*

15. April 2, Tues., *La sonnambula*

16. April 3, Wed., *Il carnivale di Venezia* (U.S. premiere)

April 4, Bklyn. Thurs., *La favorita*

17. April 5, Fri., *Il carnivale di Venezia*

April 6, Sat. matinee, *Fra Diavolo*

18. April 8, Mon., *Il carnivale di Venezia*
19. April 9, Tues., *Il carnivale di Venezia*
20. April 10, Wed., *Lucrezia Borgia*
    April 11, Bklyn. Thurs., *Il carnivale di Venezia*
21. April 12, Fri., *L'Africana* (with C. Poch as Selika)
    April 13, Sat. matinee, *Il carnivale di Venezia*
22. April 15, Mon., *L'Africana*
23. April 16, Tues., *Crispino e la comare* (by general request)
24. April 17, Wed., *Zampa*
    April 18, Bklyn. Thurs., *Faust*
    No performance Friday (Good Friday)
    April 20, Sat. matinee, *La stella del Nord*
25. April 22, Mon., *L'Africana*
26. April 23, Tues., *Faust*
    No performance Wednesday (ball for orphan asylum)
27. April 25, Thurs., *La sonnambula* (U.S. debut of Peralta)
28. April 26, Fri., *I puritani* (with Peralta)
    April 27, Sat. a.m., *L'Africana*
    April 27, Bklyn. Sat. evening, *Il carnivale di Venezia*
29. April 29, Mon., *Il carnivale di Venezia* (by general desire)
30. April 30, Tues., *Lucia di Lammermoor* (Peralta's last appearance)
    May 1, Wed., *Il barbiere di Siviglia* (Kellogg benefit)
    May 2, Bklyn. Thurs., *I puritani* (with Peralta)
    May 3, Fri., *Linda di Chamounix* (G. Ronconi benefit and last appearance)
    May 4, Sat. matinee, *La sonnambula* (with Peralta)

Fall, September 23-December 7

1st series:

1. September 23, Mon., *Don Giovanni* (with Parepa-Rosa)
2. September 24, Tues., *I puritani* (with Peralta)
3. September 25, Wed., *Otello* (with Parepa-Rosa; Pancani debut)
   September 26, Bklyn. Thurs., *Don Giovanni*
4. September 27, Fri., *Il barbiere di Siviglia* (with Peralta; Paolo Medini debut [Basilio])
   September 28, Sat. matinee, *Don Giovanni* (with Parepa-Rosa)
5. September 30, Mon., *Norma* (with Parepa-Rosa)
6. October 1, Tues., *Crispino e la comare* (with Peralta)
7. October 2, Wed., *Il trovatore*
   October 3, Bklyn. Thurs., *I puritani*
8. October 4, Fri., *Faust* (with Hauk)
   October 5, Sat. matinee, *Norma*

9. October 7, Mon., *Ernani* (with Parepa-Rosa)
10. October 8, Tues., *Lucia di Lammermoor* (with Peralta)
    No performance Wednesday (debut of Fanny Janauschek, German tragedienne, who will alternate with opera; opera: Mon., Wed., Fri.; German drama: Tues., Thurs., Sat. night)
    October 10, Bklyn. Thurs., *Otello*
11. October 11, Fri., *Gli Ugonotti*
    October 12, Sat. matinee, *Crispino e la comare*
12. October 14, Mon., *Gli Ugonotti*
13. October 16, Wed., *Gli Ugonotti*
    October 17, Bklyn. Thurs., *Faust*
14. October 18, Fri., *Don Bucefalo* (U.S. premiere)
    October 19, Sat. matinee, *Gli Ugonotti*
15. October 21, Mon., *Don Giovanni* (*Don Bucefalo* announced, but Peralta indisposed)
    Opera this week: Mon., Tues., Wed., Fri.; German drama: Thurs. and Sat.
16. October 22, Tues., *Il trovatore*
17. October 23, Wed., *Faust*
    October 24, Bklyn. Thurs., *Gli Ugonotti*
18. October 25, Fri., *Don Bucefalo*
    October 26, Sat. matinee, *Faust*
19. October 28, Mon., *Gli Ugonotti*
20. October 29, Tues., *Don Bucefalo* (*Norma* announced, but Parepa-Rosa ill)

2nd series:

1. October 30, Wed., *L'Africana*: debut of Mme. Louisa Kapp-Young (Selilka)
   October 31, Bklyn. Thurs., *Don Bucefalo*
2. November 1, Fri., *L'Africana*
   November 2, Sat. matinee, *Don Bucefalo*
   No opera at Academy this week; need to rehearse *Romeo e Giulietta*
3. November 15, Fri., *Romeo e Giulietta* (U.S. premiere; in Italian: English and German later; with Hauk [Giulietta] and Pancani [Romeo])
   November 16, Sat. matinee, *Don Pasquale*
   No performance November 18, Mon., *Romeo e Giulietta* cancelled, after about 100 persons had taken their seats
   No performance November 19, Tues., *La favorita* cancelled
   No performance November 20, Wed., season cancelled because of dispute with male chorus over salary
4. November 25, Mon., *Romeo e Giulietta*
5. November 26, Tues., *Il barbiere di Siviglia* (with Parepa-Rosa and Ronconi [Figaro])
6. November 27, Wed., *Romeo e Giulietta*
   No performance November 28, Thurs. Thanksgiving

7. November 29, Fri., *Romeo e Giulietta*

November 30, Sat. matinee, *La favorita* (*Il barbiere di Siviglia* announced; last appearance of Parepa-Rosa)

November 30, Sat. evening, last night of Fanny Janauschek

8. December 2, Mon., *Crispino e la comare*
9. December 4, Wed., *Il trovatore*

December 5, Bklyn. Thurs., *Romeo e Giulietta*

10. December 6, Fri., *Linda di Chamounix*

December 7, Sat. matinee, *Il barbiere di Siviglia*, followed by selections from *Romeo e Giulietta* (positively last appearance of Parepa-Rosa)

Appendix 2

REPERTORY

Max Maretzek's Opera Companies
1863-67

NEW YORK AND BROOKLYN ACADEMIES OF MUSIC
(INCLUDING NEW YORK WINTER GARDEN THEATRE, FALL 1866)

New York Evening	New York Saturday Matinee	Brooklyn Thursday Evening
Auber, Daniel-François-Esprit, 1782-1871		
Fra Diavolo		
1864 December 21, 23, 26, 28-29		
1865 February 3, 14	November 25	February 9
March 15, 23 (matinee)		November 23
November 10, 15		
1866 February 16	December 15	April 12
April 6		October 12, Fri.
November 28		
1867 March 8	April 6	January 31
Bellini, Vincenzo, 1801-35		
Norma		
1863 March 23, 27	October 10, eve.	November 28, Sat. eve.
April 1, 17		
October 12		
November 9		
1864 February 8	February 20	February 11
December 27, 30		
1865 February 8		February 16

New York Evening	New York Saturday Matinee	Brooklyn Thursday Evening
March 16		October 26
October 20		
November 14		
1866	February 3	
1867 March 19	March 23	March 21
September 30	October 5	

I puritani

1864 February 22		
1865 March 17		April 10, Mon.
October 10		
1866 February 5		
1867 April 26		May 2
September 24		October 3

La sonnambula

1863 November 13	November 28	
1864 February 25	April 23	
1865 March 1		
November 24		
1866 February 28		February 22
December 21		October 13, Sat. eve.
1867 April 2, 25	May 4	

Cagnoni, Antonio, 1828-96
Don Bucefalo

1867 October 18, 25, 29	November 2	October 31

Donizetti Gaetano, 1797-1848
Don Pasquale

1866 March 7	March 3	
1867	November 16	March 14

Don Sebastiano

1864 November 25, 28-29	December 17, 24	December 3, Sat. eve.
December 2, 6, 9, 14, 19		December 22

New York Evening	New York Saturday Matinee	Brooklyn Thursday Evening
1865 February 2, 20		
March 21		
1866 February 13-14, 23		March 1

L'elisir d'amore

1866		November 6, Tues.
		November 29

La favorita

1863 March 20		
1866 February 26	March 10	
March 2		
April 11		
1867 March 12	March 16	April 4
	November 30	

La figlia del reggimento

1864 December 5	December 10	
1865 March 20		March 2

Linda di Chamounix

1863 March 25	April 4	
1864 November 15		
1865		February 26, Sat. eve.
		March 11, Sat. eve.
1867 May 3		
December 6		

Lucia di Lammermoor

1863 March 31	April 11	
	November 7	
1864 February 26		April 7
October 7		
1865 February 15	February 18	
October 18		
1867 March 25		
April 30		
October 8		

New York Evening	New York Saturday Matinee	Brooklyn Thursday Evening

Lucrezia Borgia

1863 November 2, 4	November 21, eve.	
1864 March 4	November 5	October 15, Sat. eve.
April 6		
October 5, 14		
1865 September 29		
October 17		
1866 April 4	April 7, 11 a.m.	
	December 8	
1867 April 10	March 9	

Poliuto

1864 February 17		October 27
October 21, 25, 28		November 26, Sat. eve.
November 14		
December 7		
1865 April 11	February 4	October 12
September 27		
1866 February 21		

Roberto Devereux

1863 October 5, 7		

Flotow, Friedrich, 1812-83
Martha

1863 October 23		October 29
November 6		
1864 March 30	February 6	
October 24		
November 23		
1865 February 21	March 4	February 23
October 13		October 19
December 5		
1866 February 12		
April 10		
1867 March 22		February 28
		March 5, Tues.

New York Evening	New York Saturday Matinee	Brooklyn Thursday Evening

Gounod, Charles-François, 1818-93
Faust

1863 November 25, 27, 30 December 25, 30		
1864 February 4, 9, 12, 19, 27 March 1, 8, 11, 28, 31 April 5, 8, 13, 15, 18, 20, 22 October 17, 19, 26 November 18, 30 December 16	March 5, 12 April 2 October 29 November 26	October 22, Sat. eve. December 8
1865 February 7, 13 March 7 September 25 November 29	September 30	March 9 September 28
1866 February 7 December 7	March 31 December 22	November 5, Mon.
1867 March 13 April 23 October 4, 23	October 26	April 18 October 17

Romeo e Giulietta

1867 November 5, 25, 27, 29		December 5

Hérold, Ferdinand, 1791-1833
Zampa

1866 December 17, 19		December 20
1867 April 17		

Meyerbeer, Giacomo, 1791-1864
L'Africana

1865 December 1, 4, 6, 8, 11-12, 15	December 2, Sat. eve. December 9, 16	December 14
1866 February 1, 6, 9, 19, 27 March 6, 13, 20	March 31, Sat. eve.	February 8 March 17, Sat. eve.
1867 April 12, 15, 22 October 30 November 1	April 27, a.m.	

New York Evening	New York Saturday Matinee	Brooklyn Thursday Evening
Roberto il diavolo		
1864 April 1, 4, 11, 14	April 16	April 19, Tues.
1865 November 3, 6		November 9
La stella del Nord		
1866 March 9, 12, 14, 26	March 17	March 15
April 13		December 6
November 30		
December 3		
1867 March 11, 20	April 20	
Gli Ugonotti		
1866 April 2-3, 9	April 14	April 7, Sat. eve.
December 5		
1867 October 11, 14, 16, 28	October 19	October 24
Mozart, Wolfgang Amadeus, 1756-91		
Don Giovanni		
1863 November 20, 23	December 26	
1864 February 3		November 3
March 9		December 15
November 2, 16, 21		
1865 March 13		March 22, Wed.
November 30		
1866	March 24, 11 a.m.	March 22
1867 March 26, 29	September 28	March 28
September 23		September 26
October 21		
Peri, Achille, 1812-80		
Giuditta		
1863 November 11	November 14, eve.	
Petrella, Errico, 1813-88		
Il carnivale di Venezia		
1867 April 3, 5, 8-9, 29	April 13	April 11, 27 Sat. eve.

New York Evening	New York Saturday Matinee	Brooklyn Thursday Evening

Jone

1863	April 6, 8, 10, 13	May 16, 23	
	May 13, 18	October 24	
	October 14, 30		
	November 18		
	December 28		
1864	February 24	February 13, eve.	
		April 9, eve.	
1865	October 2-3	October 14	October 5
	November 1		
1866	March 19	February 24, 11 a.m.	

Ricci, Luigi, 1805-59, and Ricci, Federico, 1809-77
Crispino e la comare

1865	October 24-25, 27, 31	November 4, 11	November 2, 18 Sat. eve.
	November 7, 13, 21, 27	December 9, eve.	December 7
1866	February 2, 20	February 10, 11 a.m.	February 15
	April 4 (matinee)		October 10, Wed.
	November 26		December 18, Tues.
	December 10, 24		
1867	March 15	October 12	
	April 16		
	October 1		
	December 2		

Rossini, Gioacchino, 1792-1868
Il barbiere di Siviglia

1863		April 18	
1866	December 12, 28		December 13
1867	March 7	December 7	February 14
	May 1		
	September 27		
	November 26		

Otello

1867	September 25		October 10

New York Evening	New York Saturday Matinee	Brooklyn Thursday Evening

Semiramide
1863   March 30

Verdi, Giuseppe, 1813-1901
Aroldo

| 1863   May 4, 6, 15 | May 9 | |

Un ballo in maschera

1863 March 9, 18	March 21	March 26
April 20		
December 23		
1864 February 15		
October 12, 18		
1865 October 6, 30		
1866 March 16		
December 26		

I due Foscari
1863   April 15
1864   February 5

Ernani

1863 March 11, 14		November 12
May 8		
October 19		
1864 March 7		
1865 February 17	March 11	February 27, Mon.
October 4, 11	October 28	November 16
November 22	November 11, eve.	
1866	February 17	November 27, Tues.
1867 April 1		
October 7		

La forza del destino

| 1865   February 24, 28 | March 18 | March 14, Tues. |
| March 3, 6, 8, 10 | | |

New York Evening	New York Saturday Matinee	Brooklyn Thursday Evening
Macbeth		
1863 October 21, 26		
November 26		
1864 March 2		
Rigoletto		
1863 October 9	October 17	October 15
1864 November 4, 22		November 19, Sat. eve.
1865 November 8		
La traviata		
1863 March 13	March 28	March 19
October 16	October 31	October 22
1864 April 21	October 15	
October 4		
1865 February 10		
October 16		
Il trovatore		
1863 March 6	March 7	
May 11		
October 28		
November 16		
1864 February 1, 29		October 6
October 3, 10, 31		
December 12		
1865 February 6		
October 9, 23		
November 17		
1866 March 5	December 1	March 8
December 14		October 11
1867 March 18	March 30	
October 2, 22		
December 4		

Appendix 3

NUMBER OF
PERFORMANCES PER OPERA

Max Maretzek's Opera Companies
1863-67

NEW YORK AND BROOKLYN ACADEMIES OF MUSIC
(INCLUDING NEW YORK WINTER GARDEN THEATRE, FALL 1866)

Composer/Title	New York	New York Saturday Matinee	Brooklyn	Total
Gounod, *Faust*	39	9	7	55
Ricci, *Crispino e la comare*	18	5	6	29
Meyerbeer, *L'Africana*	20	5	3	28
Verdi, *Il trovatore*	20	3	3	26
Bellini, *Norma*	15	5	5	25
Petrella, *Jone*	15	7	1	23
Auber, *Fra Diavolo*	15	3	5	23
Mozart, *Don Giovanni*	13	3	6	22
Donizetti, *Don Sebastiano*	14	2	3	19
Verdi, *Ernani*	11	4	4	19
Flotow, *Martha*	11	2	5	18
Donizetti, *Lucrezia Borgia*	10	5	1	16
Verdi, *Un ballo in maschera*	11	1	1	13
Meyerbeer, *La stella del Nord*	9	2	2	13
Donizetti, *Poliuto*	9	1	3	13
Bellini, *La sonnambula*	8	3	2	13
Donizetti, *Lucia di Lammermoor*	8	3	1	12
Meyerbeer, *Gli Ugonotti*	8	2	2	12
Verdi, *La traviata*	6	3	2	11
Rossini, *Il barbiere di Siviglia*	6	2	2	10

Composer/Title	New York	New York Saturday Matinee	Brooklyn	Total
Meyerbeer, *Roberto il diavolo*	6	1	2	9
Bellini, *I puritani*	6	0	3	9
Donizetti, *La favorita*	5	3	1	9
Verdi, *La forza del destino*	6	1	1	8
Petrella, *Il carnivale di Venezia**	5	1	2	8
Donizetti, *Linda di Chamounix*	4	1	2	7
Verdi, *Rigoletto*	4	1	2	7
Gounod, *Romeo e Giulietta**	4	0	1	5
Cagnoni, *Don Bucefalo**	3	1	1	5
Verdi, *Macbeth*	4	0	0	4
Verdi, *Aroldo*	3	1	0	4
Hérold, *Zampa*	3	0	1	4
Donizetti, *La figlia del reggimento*	2	1	1	4
Donizetti, *Don Pasquale*	1	2	1	4
Donizetti, *Roberto Devereux*	2	0	0	2
Verdi, *I due Foscari*	2	0	0	2
Peri, *Giuditta*	1	1	0	2
Rossini, *Otello*	1	0	1	2
Donizetti, *L'elisir d'amore*	0	0	2	2
Rossini, *Semiramide*	1	0	0	1

* Premiered 1867 (therefore few performances given).

Appendix 4

FURTHER REVELATIONS
MARETZEK REPERTORY

Performances at the Metropolitan Opera
1883-2005

THE METROPOLITAN OPERA, NEW YORK*

Ranking**	Work	Performances	First/Last
4	Verdi, *La traviata*	903	1883-2004
7	Verdi, *Rigoletto*	791	1883-2004
8	Gounod, *Faust*	722	1883-2005
12	Verdi, *Il trovatore*	599	1883-2003
13	Rossini, *Il barbiere di Siviglia*	550	1883-2005
14	Donizetti, *Lucia di Lammermoor*	548	1883-2003
16	Mozart, *Don Giovanni*	496	1883-2005
24	Gounod, *Romeo e Giulietta* (in French)	300	1884-1998
26	Verdi, *Un ballo in maschera*	278	1889-2005
32	Donizetti, *L'elisir d'amore*	247	1904-99
37	Verdi, *La forza del destino*	220	1918-96
48	Bellini, *Norma*	139	1890-2001
49	Meyerbeer, *Gli Ugonotti* (in French)	129	1884-1915
53	Flotow, *Martha*	116	1884-1968
54	Donizetti, *Don Pasquale*	115	1899-1980
60	Donizetti, *La figlia del reggimento*	88	1902-95
63	Verdi, *Ernani*	81	1903-85

* Data from MetOpera Database; The Metropolitan Opera Archives (http://66.187.153.86/archives/frame.htm).

** Rankings (assigned by the editor) are approximate because operas having the same number of performances are listed alphabetically within that category in the Met database. Thirteen operas, for example, have been performed nine times, so they are ranked 184-196, depending on where they fall alphabetically.

Ranking	Work	Performances	First/Last
65	Verdi, *Macbeth*	80	1959-88
68	Meyerbeer, *L'Africana* (in French)	71	1888-1934
76	Bellini, *La sonnambula*	65	1883-1972
97	Bellini, *I puritani*	42	1883-1997
114	Rossini, *Semiramide*	28	1892-1993
116	Donizetti, *La favorita*	25	1895-1978
186	Auber, *Fra Diavolo*	9	1902-10
204	Donizetti, *Linda di Chamounix*	8	1934-35
217	Meyerbeer, *Roberto il diavolo* (in French)	7	1883-84
261	Ricci, *Crispino e la comare*	4	1919
311	Donizetti, *Lucrezia Borgia*	1	1904

Never performed at the Met:

Cagnoni, *Don Bucefalo*

Donizetti, *Don Sebastiano*

Donizetti, *Poliuto*

Donizetti, *Roberto Devereux*

Hérold, *Zampa*

Meyerbeer, *La stella del Nord*

Peri, *Giuditta*

Petrella, *Il carnivale di Venezia*

Petrella, *Jone*

Rossini, *Otello*

Verdi, *Aroldo*

Verdi, *I due Foscari*

Bibliography

Abbott, Mabel. "Musical Traditions in Old Homes." *New York Sun*, 28 September 1929, p. 24.

Account of the Terrific and Fatal Riot at the New-York Astor Place Opera House. New York: H.M. Ranney, 1849. Reprint, New York: Museum of the City of New York, 1999.

Ahlquist, Karen. *Democracy at the Opera: Music, Theater, and Culture in New York City, 1815-60.* Urbana: University of Illinois Press, 1997.

Album pintoresco de la isla de Cuba. Havana: B. May, 1853.

Arditi, Luigi. *My Reminiscences.* New York: Dodd Mead, 1896. Reprint, New York: Da Capo, 1977.

Barnum, P.T. *Life of P.T. Barnum.* New York: Redfield, 1855.

Berlioz, Hector. *Memoirs, 1803-1865.* Trans. and ed. David Cairns. New York: Norton, 1975.

Bethell, Leslie. *Cuba: A Short History.* Cambridge: Cambridge University Press, 1993.

Blair, John Purdy. "Productions at Niblo's Garden Theatre, 1849-1862." Ph.D. diss, University of Georgia, 1986.

Brasker, Thomas L. *Whitman as Editor of the Brooklyn Daily Eagle.* Detroit: Wayne State University Press, 1970.

Brooklyn Eagle. Brooklyn, 1841-1955.

Brown, T. Allston. *A History of the New York Stage from the First Performance in 1732-1901.* 3 vols. New York: Dodd, Mead, 1903.

Buckley, Peter George. "To the Opera House: Culture and Society in New York City, 1820-1860." Ph.D. diss., State University of New York at Stony Brook, 1984.

Bull, Inez. *Ole Bull's Activities in the United States between 1843 and 1880: A Biography.* Smithtown, New York: Exposition, 1982.

Burrows, Edwin G., and Mike Wallace. *Gotham, A History of New York City to 1898.* New York: Oxford, 1999.

Carpentier, Alejo. "Music in Cuba, 1523-1900." *Musical Quarterly* 33 (1947): 365-80.

_____. *La música en Cuba.* Havana: Editorial letras cubanas, 1979.

Cone, John Frederick. *First Rival of the Metropolitan Opera.* New York: Columbia University Press, 1983.

Costello, Augustine E. *Our Firemen, A History of the New York Fire Departments, Volunteer and Paid.* New York: A. E. Costello, 1887.

Cropsey, Eugene H. *Crosby's Opera House: Symbol of Chicago's Cultural Awakening.* Madison: Fairleigh Dickinson University Press, 1999.

Crouthamel, James L. *Bennett's New York Herald and the Rise of the Popular Press.* Syracuse: Syracuse University Press, 1989.

Crow, Duncan. *Henry Wikoff, the American Chevalier.* London: MacGibbon & Kee, 1963.

Cumberland, Charles C. *Mexico, the Struggle for Modernity.* London: Oxford University Press, 1968.

"Current History and Opinion: Max Maretzek." *The Chautauquan* 25 (July 1897): 423.

Delarue, Allison. *The Chevalier Henry Wikoff: Impresario, 1840.* Princeton: privately printed at the Princeton University Press, 1968.

Del Grosso, George. Private collection, New York City.

Díaz Ayala, Cristóbal. *Música cubana del areyto a la nueva trova.* Miami: Ediciones Universal, 1981.

District of Columbia Historical Records Survey. *Bio-Bibliographical Index of Musicians in the United States of America since Colonial Times.* Washington, D.C.: Music Section, Pan American Union, 1956.

Dizikes, John. *Opera in America: A Cultural History.* New Haven: Yale University Press, 1993.

Dwight's Journal of Music: A Paper of Art and Literature. Boston (weekly): ed. John Sullivan Dwight, 1852-81.

"The Era of National Expansion." In *Grove's Dictionary of Music and Musicians: American Supplement.* Philadelphia: T. Presser, 1920.

Faner, Robert D. *Walt Whitman & Opera.* Philadelphia: University of Pennsylvania Press, 1951.

Fermer, Douglas. *James Gordon Bennett and the New York Herald.* New York: St. Martin's, 1986.

Franz, William C. "Island Man Brought Opera to U.S.A." *Staten Island Register,* 16 October 1980, pp. 1, 8.

Garibaldi-Meucci Museum, owned and operated by the Order, Sons of Italy in America. http://www.garibaldimeuccimuseum.org, 7 April 2003.

Gerson, Robert A. *Music in Philadelphia.* Westport, CT: Greenwood, 1970.

Glackens, Ira. *Yankee Diva: Lillian Nordica and the Golden Days of Opera.* New York: Coleridge, 1963.

Goldin, Milton. *The Music Merchants.* London: Macmillan, 1969.

Grant, Mark N. *Maestros of the Pen: A History of Classical Music Criticism in America.* Boston: Northeastern University Press, 1998.

Grau, Robert. *Forty Years Observation of Music and the Drama.* New York: Broadway Publishing, 1909.

Guanche, Jesús. "Teatros: Cuba." In *Diccionario de la música española e hispano-americana*, 10:218-21. Madrid: Sociedad General de la Autores y Editores, 1999-2002.

Hanna, Alfred Jackson, and Kathryn Abbey Hanna. *Napoleon III and Mexico*. Chapel Hill: University of North Carolina Press, 1971.

Hauk, Minnie. *Memories of a Singer*. London: A.M. Philpot, 1925. Reprint, New York: Arno, 1977.

Haywood, Charles. Introduction to *Revelations of an Opera Manager in 19ᵗʰ Century America*, by Max Maretzek. New York: Dover, 1968.

Hazard, Samuel. *Cuba with Pen and Pencil*. Hartford: Hartford Pub. Co., 1871.

Henderson, Ruth. "A Confluence of Moravian Impresarios: Max Maretzek, the Strakosches, and the Graus." In *Importing Culture: European Music and Musicians in New York, 1840-1890*, ed. John Graziano. Rochester: University of Rochester Press, 2006, in press.

Hipsher, Edward Ellsworth. *American Opera and Its Composers*. Philadelphia: T. Presser, 1934.

Hoole, William Stanley. *The Ante-Bellum Charleston Theatre*. University: University of Alabama Press, 1946.

Howard, Ida. "A Prima Donna of the Old Days: Madame Maretzek's Reminiscences of the Opera Stage." *San Francisco Chronicle*, 1 February 1903, p. 8.

Iggers, Wilma, ed. *The Jews of Bohemia and Moravia*. Detroit: Wayne State University Press, 1992.

Jackson, Kenneth. *The Encyclopedia of New York City*. New Haven: Yale University Press, 1995.
    S.v. "Ladies' Mile," by Amanda Aaron.
    S.v. "Paving," by Craig D. Bida.
    S.v. "Population," by Nathan Kantrowitz.
    S.v. "Skyscrapers, 1870-1916," by Sarah Bradford Landau.
    S.v. "Subways," by Peter Derrick.

Jacobsen, Anita Kershaw. "Max Maretzek, Staten Islander." *The Staten Island Historian* 5, no. 3 (July-September 1942): 17-18, 23-24.

Kaufman, Thomas G. *Verdi and His Major Contemporaries*. New York: Garland, 1990.

Kellogg, Clara Louise. *Memoirs of an American Prima Donna*. New York: Knickerbocker, 1913. Reprint, New York: Da Capo, 1978.

Kieval, Hillel J. *The Making of Czech Jewry: National Conflict in Bohemia, 1870-1918*. New York: Oxford University Press, 1988.

Krehbiel, Henry Edward. *Chapters of Opera*. New York: H. Holt, 1908. Reprint, New York: Da Capo, 1980.

————. *More Chapters of Opera*. New York: H. Holt, 1919. Reprint, Westport, CT: Hyperion, 1980.

Lahee, Henry C. *Grand Opera in America*. Boston: Page, 1902. Reprint, Freeport, NY: Books for Libaries, 1971.

————. *The Grand Opera Singers of Today*. Boston: Page, 1922.

Lane, Wheaton J. *Commodore Vanderbilt: An Epic of the Steam Age*. New York: Alfred Knopf, 1942.

Lawrence, Vera Brodsky. *Strong on Music*. Vol. 1: New York: Oxford, 1988; vols. 2-3: Chicago: University of Chicago Press, 1995, 1999.

Lerner, Lawrence. "The Rise of the Impresario: Bernard Ullman and the Transformation of Musical Culture in Nineteenth Century America." Ph.D. diss., University of Wisconsin, 1970.

Lindsay, Antoinette Maretzek. "Last Will and Testament." New York County: 11 May 1944.

Loewenberg, Alfred. *Annals of Opera, 1597-1940*. 3rd rev. ed. Totowa, NJ: Rowman & Littlefield, 1978.

McConachie, Bruce A. "New York Operagoing, 1825-50: Creating an Elite Social Ritual." *American Music* 6, no. 2 (summer 1988): 181-92.

McKnight, Mark C. "Music Criticism in *The New York Times* and *The New York Tribune*, 1851-1876." Ph.D. diss., Louisiana State University, 1980.

Madeira, Louis C. *Annals of Music in Philadelphia and History of the Musical Fund Society from its Organization in 1820 to the Year 1858*. Philadelphia: Lippincott, 1896. Reprint, New York: Da Capo, 1973.

Maretzek, Max. *Crotchets and Quavers: or Revelations of an Opera Manager in America*. New York: French, 1855. Reprints: New York: Da Capo, 1966; New York: Dover (under alternate title, *Revelations of an Opera Manager in 19th-Century America*), 1968.

————. *Sharps and Flats*. New York: American Musician Pub., 1890. Reprint, New York: Dover (with *Crotchets and Quavers*, under alternate title, as noted above), 1968.

Martens, Frederick H. "Max Maretzek." In *Dictionary of American Biography* 12, p. 281. New York: Scribners, 1933.

Martin, E.S. "This Busy World." *Harper's Weekly* 41 (29 May 1897): 535.

Mathews, W.S.B. *A Hundred Years of Music in America*. Chicago: G.L. Howe, 1889. Reprint, New York: AMS Press, 1970.

Mattfeld, Julius. *A Handbook of American Operatic Premieres, 1731-1962*. Detroit Studies in Music Bibliography, no. 5. Detroit: Information Service, 1963.

————. *A Hundred Years of Grand Opera in New York, 1825-1925: A Record of Performances*. New York: New York Public Library, 1927.

"Max and Madame Maretzek." *Cincinnati Enquirer*, 16 October 1881, p. 12.

"Max Maretzek." (Portraits of the People, no. 326.) Unidentified New York publication, probably fall 1849, collection PR 52, Box 90, Folder Mare-Mare misc., New-York Historical Society.

"Max's Memories." *American Art Journal* 59 (30 April 1892): 93-94.

Metropolitan Opera. "MetOpera Database; The Metropolitan Opera Archives." http://66.187.153.86/archives/frame.htm,1 June 2005.

Meyer, Michael C. *The Course of Mexican History*. New York: Oxford University Press, 1991.

Miller, Philip. "Opera the Story of an Immigrant." In *One Hundred Years of Music in America*, ed. Paul Henry Lang, pp. 53-79. New York: G. Schirmer, 1961.

Miller, Robert Ryal. *Mexico: A History*. Norman: University of Oklahoma Press, 1985.

Moody, Richard. *The Astor Place Riot*. Bloomington: Indiana University Press, 1958.

The New Grove Dictionary of American Music (1986).

    S.v. "Criticism: 1850 to World War I," by Edward O.D. Downes.

The New Grove Dictionary of Music and Musicians, Second ed. (2001).

    S.v. "Havana," by Robert Stevenson and Victoria Eli Rodriguez.

    S.v. "Clara Louise Kellogg," by H. Wiley Hitchcock and Katherine K. Preston.

    S.v. "Emanuele Muzio," by Gustavo Marchesi.

    S.v. "Jaime Nuno," by Robert Stevenson.

    S.v. "Puebla (de los Angeles)," by Alice Ray Catalyne.

    S.v. "Santiago de Cuba," by Robert Stevenson and Robin Moore.

The New Grove Dictionary of Opera (1992).

    S.v. *"Ballo in maschera,"* by Roger Parker.

New York City directories. New York: Doggett/Rode, 1851-61.

New York (NY) Courts. Supreme Court. "Max Maretzek, respondent, against William Cauldwell and Horace P. Whitney, appellants." New York: Wyn Koop & Hallenbeck, 1867.

New York Herald. Ed. James Gordon Bennett, Sr. New York, 1835-1924.

New York Philharmonic Archives. Harold Lineback Collection, visited 30 April 2003; 10 May 2005.

New York Public Library. Manuscripts and Archives Division. Letters of Adelaide Phillipps, mainly to Mrs. Gordon Lester Ford.

New York Times. Ed. Henry Jarvis Raymond. New York, 1851-.

New York Tribune. Ed. Horace Greeley. New York, 1841-1924.

Notable American Women, ed. Edward T. James. Cambridge, MA: Belknap, 1971.

    S.v. "Minnie Hauk," by Francis D. Perkins.

    S.v. "Lillian Nordica," by William Lichtenwanger.

    S.v. "Adelaide Phillipps," by Victor Fell Yellin.

Odell, George. *Annals of the New York Stage*. 15 vols. New York: Columbia University Press, 1927-49. Reprint, New York: AMS Press, 1970.

Olavarria y Ferrari, Enrique de. *Reseña histórica del teatro en México, 1538-1911*. Third ed., 5 vols. México: Editorial Porrúa, 1961.

Orovio, Helio. *Cuban Music from A to Z*. Durham: Duke University Press, 2004.

Orr, N. Lee. *Alfredo Barili and the Rise of Classical Music in Atlanta*. Atlanta: Scholars Press, 1996.

Orta Velázquez, Guillermo. *Breve historia de la música en México*. Mexico: Libreria de M. Porrua, 1971.

Patrick, Douglas. "Stapleton Man Hits High C with Historic Find." *Staten Island Advance*, 13 December 1981, pp. A1, A4.

Phillips-Matz, Mary Jane. *Verdi, a Biography*. New York: Oxford University Press, 1993.

Pleasants, Henry. *The Great Singers*. New York: Simon & Schuster, 1966.

Preston, Katherine K. "Max Maretzek." In *American National Biography*, 14:502-04. New York: Oxford University Press, 1999.

————. *Opera on the Road: Traveling Opera Troupes in the United States, 1825-60*. Urbana: University of Illinois Press, 1993.

Pride, Leo B., ed. *International Theatre Directory: A World Directory*. New York: Simon & Schuster, 1973.

"The Progress of the World: The Month's Death Roll." *Review of Reviews* 15 (June 1897): 661.

"Retirement of Max Maretzek." *The Spirit of the Times* (New York) 87 (27 June 1874): 500.

Revilla, Manuel G. "Cenobia Paniagua." *Revista musical mexicana* 2 (1942): 178-82, 202-4, 216, 234, 251-52.

Reycraft, Jack. "Back when Verdi was Young." *Staten Island Advance*, 2 February 1965, p. 16.

————. "A Monument to Melody." *Staten Island Advance*, 30 June 1967, p. 14.

————. "Operatic Pioneer an Islander." *Staten Island Advance*, 28 October 1979, p. 8.

Richmond County Real Estate Records. (Property Records Office, 130 Stuyvesant Place, Staten Island.)

Root, Deane L. *American Popular Stage Music, 1860-1880*. Ann Arbor: UMI, 1981.

Rosenthal, Harold, ed. *The Mapleson Memoirs: The Career of an Operatic Impresario, 1858-1888*. New York: Appleton-Century, 1966.

Rosselli, John. *The Opera Industry in Italy from Cimarosa to Verdi: The Role of the Impresario*. Cambridge: Cambridge University Press, 1984.

Rubin, Libby Antarsh. "Gottschalk in Cuba." Ph.D. diss., Columbia University, 1974.

Russell, Frank. *Queen of Song: The Life of Henrietta Sontag*. New York: Exposition, 1964.

Saffle, Michael, ed. *Music and Culture in America, 1861-1919*. New York: Garland, 1998.

Sayer, Derek. *The Coasts of Bohemia: A Czech History*. Princeton: Princeton University Press, 1998.

Schattschneider, David A. "Moravians." In *The Encyclopedia of Religion*, 10:106-8. New York: Macmillan, 1986-87.

Schmelz, U.O., P. Glickson, and S. Della Pergola. *Papers in Jewish Demography, 1973*. Jerusalem: Institute of Contemporary Jewry, 1977.

Schonberg, Harold C. "The Don Quixote of Opera." *American Heritage* 27 (February 1976): 48-56, 97.

Smith, Dorothy Valentine. *Staten Island, Gateway to New York*. Philadelphia: Chilton, 1970.

Smith, Mortimer B. *The Life of Ole Bull*. Princeton: American Scandinavian Foundation, 1943. Reprint, Westport, CT: Greenwood, 1973.

Starr, S. Frederick. *Bamboula! The Life and Times of Louis Moreau Gottschalk*. New York: Oxford University Press, 1995.

Stevenson, E. "Music and Drama." *Harper's Weekly* 41 (10 July 1897): 686.

Stevenson, Robert. *Music in Mexico, a Historical Survey*. New York: Thomas Y. Crowell, 1952.

Strakosch, Maurice. *Souvenirs d'un impresario*. Paris: Ollendorff, 1887.

————. "Strakosch and Patti." (Abridgement and English trans. of his *Souvenirs d'un impresario*.) *Musical Courier* 41, no. 17, whole no. 1074 (24 October 1900): 26-36.

Strakosch, Max. Unpublished memoirs. Harold Lineback Collection, New York Philharmonic Archives.

Tagliafico, Joseph (Dieudonné). "Letter to a French Friend in Cuba." *The Musical World* (London) 36, no. 50 (11 December 1858): 797-98.

Teran, Jay Robert. "The New York Opera Audience, 1825-1974." Ph.D. diss., New York University, 1974.

Thompson, Oscar. *The American Singer: A Hundred Years of Success in Opera*. New York: Dial, 1937.

Waterston, Anna Cabot Lowell Quincy. *Adelaide Phillipps*. Boston: A. Williams, 1883.

White, Richard Grant. "Opera in New York." *Century Illustrated Monthly Magazine* 23 (March 1882): 686-703, (April 1882): 865-82; 24 (May 1882): 31-43, (June 1882): 193-210.

Wilbur, Marie A. "Last Will and Testament." Staten Island: Surrogate Court, County of Richmond, 9 October 1944.

Index

Note: page numbers in boldface indicate illustrations.